How to Make the Internet Work for You

Surprisingly Simple Ways to Turn Clicks into Local Clients

An Essential Guide for Getting More Clients by Using the Internet

By

William H. Hawthorn

How to Make the Internet Work for You!

Surprisingly Simple Ways to Turn Clicks into Local Clients
An Essential Guide for Getting More Clients through the Internet

By William H. Hawthorn

PUBLISHER:

United States Edition- contains US publications.

Limit of Liability Disclaimer: The information contained in this book is for information purposes only and may not apply to your situation. The author, publisher, distributor and provider provide no warranty about the content or accuracy of content enclosed. Information provided is subjective. Keep this in mind when reviewing this guide.

Neither the publisher nor author shall be liable for any loss of profit or any other commercial damages resulting from use of this guide. All links are for information purposes only and are not warranted for content, accuracy or any other implied or explicit purpose.

Earnings Disclaimer: All income examples in this book are just that, examples. They are not intended to represent or guarantee that everyone will achieve the same results. Each individual's success will be determined by his or her desire, dedication, background, effort and motivation to work. There is no guarantee you will duplicate any of the results stated here. You recognize that any business endeavor has an inherent risk for loss of capital.

The "typical" result one can expect to achieve is nothing. The "typical" person never gets to the end of this book. The "typical" person fails to implement anything. Thus they earn nothing. Zero. No income. Perhaps even a loss of income. "Typical" people do nothing and therefore they achieve nothing.

Be atypical. Do something. Implement something. If it doesn't work, make a change...and implement that. Try again...try harder. Persist. Then reap the rewards.

ISBN-13:
978-1494985868

ISBN-10:
1494985861

Your book has been assigned a CreateSpace ISBN.
Published in the United States of America

Table of Contents

Introduction

You may ask me, "What gives you the right to give advice?"

I am one of those persistent guys that spent tens of thousands of hard earned dollars trying to figure it out. Much like yourself, possibly? Maybe you have not spent "tens of thousands," but I would bet you have spent your share.

When I first started to consult other business owners (like me), I started to notice how little most business owners knew about marketing or about how to promote their products or services. Actually, it seemed outrageous that this could be the case.

I mean, most of these folks were extremely good at the "technical" stuff, but they had no clue about how to get with prospects who would want to purchase their product or service. In fact, most of these folks didn't even know who their ideal prospect or customer was.

I thought, if you wanted to make money, wouldn't it help to find out who and where these prospects were? I mean, wouldn't that make sense?

So I went to work on my own business as the "marketeer." This was not like the Three Musketeers, though. I was by myself, without the other two. But I was willing to make the journey alone.

Over a thirty year time period, I created a thriving business -- only to get to the end and sell the real estate the business was on. That allowed me to move on to my second career: consulting and speaking.

Over the past five years, I have consulted hundreds of businesses and spoken to thousands of businessmen. I've acquired some simple "laws" that need to be in place for anyone to be a successful "marketeer."

This book has some of my latest shortcuts and ideas that will help you find those prospects who can then become your loyal customers. I have been successful at mentoring, coaching and consulting business owners in how to organize production, position themselves as industry leaders, market their way to success, and achieve sales that fill their checkbooks beyond expectation.

But my favorite is thing the marketing. Especially the online stuff. Hence, this book. It will help you get familiar with me and find out how I may be able to help you now or some day in the future.

So find a comfortable spot, grab a note pad, and let's start our journey together . . .

Customer Journey Example: Car Purchase

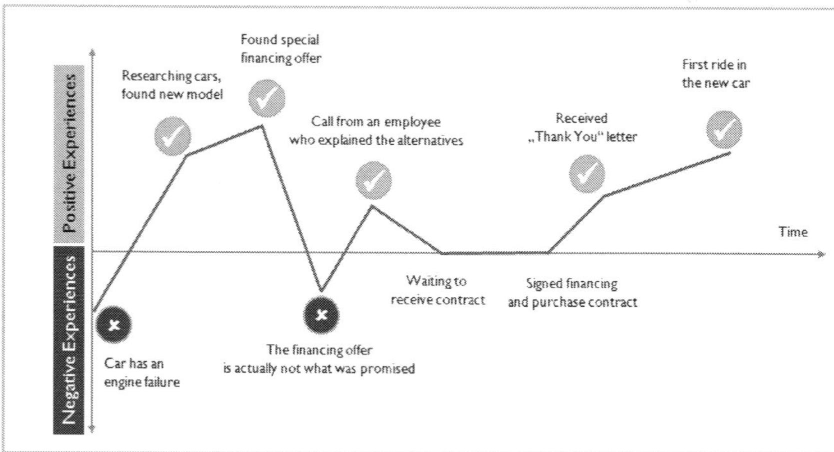

Customer Journey Example: For The Internet

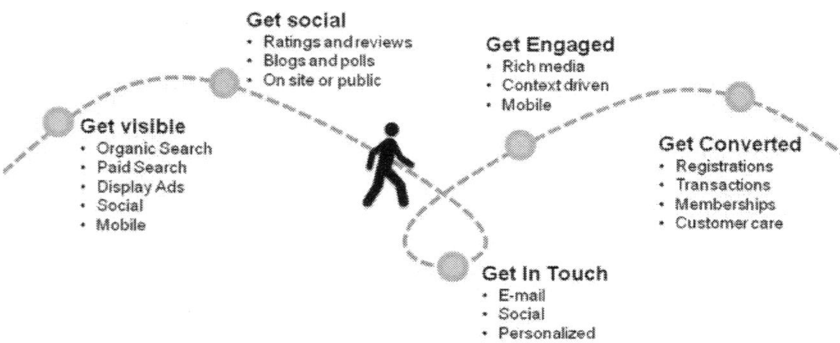

The Internet?

A book about the Internet? At first, it didn't make sense. The Internet changes every day… but once this book is printed, it will be around forever.

It's true: the Internet is fluid, and things do change from time to time. However, there are tried and true principles that will never change. In fact, they will only increase in their effectiveness as the Internet grows and as traditional advertising fades away.

This book has the best of both worlds. Internet plus a traditional "think" behind it.

What you will find here are the stable principles. In other words, they work. When you implement them. They are based on the rock-solid strategies that I have been using successfully with clients for years.

The results speak for themselves.

Of course, there are some surface elements that do change from time to time, and when I came across one of those, I decided to add an online section of this book for those of you who want the latest and the greatest. Just look for the big boxes that say "Free Resource." They will take you to a page on a website where some of my friends host the most current data on a particular topic.

One piece of advice: use these resources. They will help you get more clients and gain more freedom.

On that note, the difference between an average business and a *great* business comes down to implementation. One business often differs from another only in the owner's willingness to implement the things that he or she has learned.

The same is true about the information in this book. It works, and similar to everything you learned in school, it works when implemented. But *only* when it's implemented. Just *knowing* all of this information won't help you make any more money or sell any more services or even sell your practice for more.

When you *implement* it, this information can make you an additional six figures or more in a year -- plus you will help more people, create a more stable business, and gain some nice bragging rights at the next conference you attend.

Use it…and send me your success stories.

One of the most common questions I get from business owners is, "How am I supposed to get all of this done?" After all, I have a business to run.

My first question to them is then: Are you in "cope" or are you organized as a business owner?

The second question is: Do you have a marketing problem or a production problem?

Some business people actually believe they have too much work and don't need to market. When digging in with them, I always find that production is actually low and is causing a "log jam." That logjam only makes it look like there is "plenty" of work.

The answer here is for smart business owners to learn how to build (or find) good teams. Then their production can be a steady stream of products (or service) flying out the door. This creates a high exchange (money for those products or services) with their customers.

The solution to a money problem is not more money invested by the owner, but more actual products or services delivered into the hands of those who want them enough to pay you for them.

It's important to note, too, that it is ultimately the *result* from the product or service that your customer or client is actually going after, not necessarily the product or service itself.

Example: Guy walks into a hardware store. Asks for a drill. Does he really want a drill? Or does he really want the hole the drill makes? If the hardware attendant were clever, he would ask the customer what he was going to use the drill for. There might be another solution for the customer than a drill. Possibly another product that could be sold instead of the drill or along with it that would provide a better solution altogether.

Now you have created a relationship with a customer who is willing to pay you well (exchange) for not only the product you've suggested, but for the service, the help, you've given.

Toward the end of the book, I have included a section on where and how to find competent people to build a team to help you implement your web strategy.

Okay. Let's get started.

GETTING STARTED

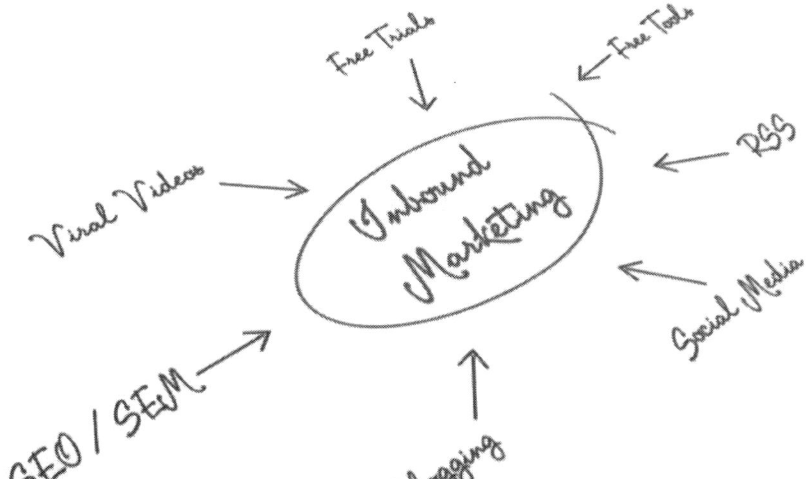

Chapter 1

Clients for Life: How to Use the Internet to Fuel Your Local Business

Congratulations!

Just by getting to this first chapter, you're already way ahead of your competition.

Why? Most people don't take the necessary action for success. It's that implementation thing. You've gotten this far, so let's go the rest of the way together.

You're forward-thinking. You know that the Internet is a big deal, and you know that even if your business is humming along very well, you might use the Internet to drum up a little more business here and there, if you can, and maybe this book can help you supplement your advertising.

Now, some of you may still think that the Internet won't help you all that much. After, all, local people know you, you're in the Yellow Pages, and you're still getting a healthy amount of business. Who searches for a local business like yours on the Internet, anyway?

The majority of your potential clients. That's who.

Google has done a great job of changing our lives with regard to this, haven't they?

Recent research shows that, increasingly, online searches are done overwhelmingly by local businesses. A 2010 study by BIA/Kelsey and the research firm ComStat found that a staggering 97% of consumers research their purchases and *local* services online before they fulfill them at a local business.

This isn't just the case with local services, either. Major e-retailers are being beaten out by customers who research products online, but choose to buy at local stores. People seem to like human interaction: they inform themselves online, but in the end they want that personal connection. That knowledgeable suggestion about a drill.

The consequence of this is that, unfortunately, any business with no (or substandard) Internet presence is left out of that potential customer's research process. People want to fulfill their online searches locally, but if you don't pop up when they're doing their research, you'll simply fly under their radar and lose their business to another business who has that Internet presence.

This is, of course, dangerous for any local business owner who has so far avoided being on the Internet or whose website is not producing results – which is the same as not being on the Internet. This may sound alarmist or nonsensical, but it's true: the majority of potential clients are looking for their representation on the Internet.

They even prefer it over more traditional media like the Yellow Pages or TV. In fact, a recent 2009 study by comScore and TMP Directional Marketing showed for the first time that the number of clients searching for local businesses on the Internet exceeded those who consulted the Yellow Pages. The Yellow Pages have been headed downhill ever since the Internet arrived. The fact of the matter is that people simply don't use the Yellow Pages anymore since the Internet is a much easier and more convenient way for them to get information.

It may seem surprising at first, but it does begin to make sense once you think about it. You can even look to your own habits as proof of this changing trend. How often do you use the Yellow Pages to find something you're looking for? Do you run over to your desk and flip through the Yellow Pages to find what you need, or do you do a quick Google search and find what you need right away?

Even if you are still a Yellow Page user, take a look at others around you, your kids, friends, family. How many of them still use the Yellow Pages? If you're honest with yourself, you won't be surprised at all to find that the way people now look for services has changed.

What is surprising, however, is how many businesses still have huge portions of their budget devoted to the Yellow Pages and print ads. Many businesses can have $20,000 or more allocated to their Yellow Page advertising budget. In this day and age that's simply a waste of money. Today the Yellow Pages are simply not returning enough business to justify that level of major investment. Virtually all businesses that can or do track ROI (Return On Investment) from print advertising campaigns have seen diminishing returns.

Every month, without fail, more people are using Google and other search engines instead of traditional media and methods of research.

This is not just some passing trend. Online search has supplanted the Yellow Pages, and it's here to stay.

An effective online presence is not just a temporary strategy. It's a forward look to a future where search engines are the main tool customers use to make their decisions.

Yellow Pages Dead?

These days, you cannot rely solely on the Yellow Pages to generate new leads. In fact, this medium is slowing dying and consumers have shifted to using "Google" to find new Contractor Services.

What That Means for You

So how do you get in on this search corner of the market?

After all, don't big businesses dominate search engine rankings on the Internet? Can local businesses even compete in this ferocious online arena?

As it turns out, they can. Google has recently made some of the most significant changes to their search algorithms (changing technical formulas used to rank search prospects) which we've seen in a long time. They've shifted searches for brick and mortar businesses to something called "local search return" or, specifically, Google Places / Google + Local. Previously, this feature had only been available on their Google Maps service.

What is local search return? Originally, when a user searched on Google Maps, local businesses would pop up in the area the user was searching in. If a user searched "New York, NY," for example, the Google interactive map that would appear also had helpful markers placed around the map which indicated the local businesses that were nearby.

Restaurants and hotels were the first businesses to jump on this feature and use it to their advantage. It was a natural fit. Visitors to a new city needed to know places to eat and sleep, and the Google Maps local search return feature helped both users and customers by showing them immediately where these local businesses were and facilitating that offline, real world conversion of a virtual searcher to a live customer.

Go to: http://www.google.com/business/placesforbusiness to see how this works (Figure on next page).

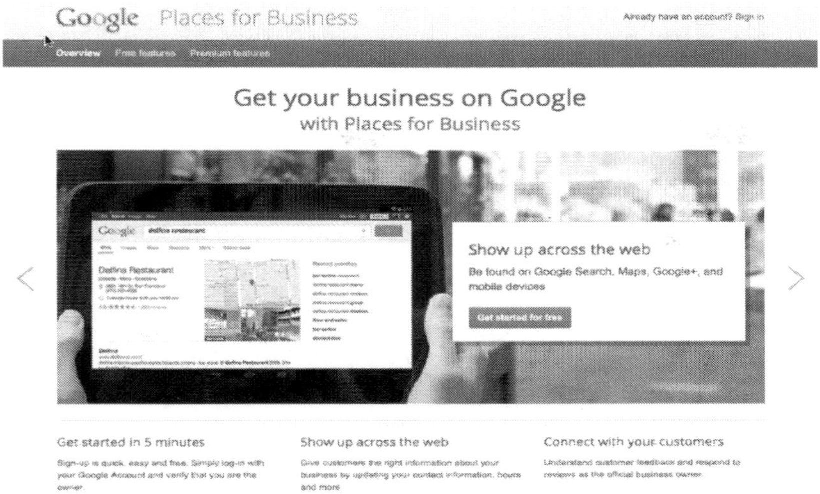

It was not long, however, before businesses besides restaurants and hotels realized that this service could benefit them, too, and they began listing themselves on the local search return maps as well. Eventually, with all this increased online activity, Google realized that if users were searching maps to get this kind of information, then probably many users were also searching in the regular search text box, as well, and had not yet realized that they had to go to the maps section to get those local search results.

Again, look at your own or your friends' search habits. How often do you go to Google Maps to search for something? Most likely, you simply type it into the Google.com search box and hit enter.

Now, up to this point in time, Google's regular search box was just returning a list of links as search results. They weren't map-based and they often weren't nearly as useful as the map results that Google Maps was returning. Then, aware of all this new activity, Google started incorporating the local search returns into their regular search page.

Today, when you search for a brick and mortar business on Google, your search returns a map, as well, with up to seven marked locations that are all local businesses.

This is great news for local businesses. Now there's a real chance for competition. A year ago -- or even six months ago -- local businesses simply couldn't compete on a national level with giants like Amazon or

Wikipedia. Today, however, there's a real chance for your business to show up in the top three results on a local search page.

This gives you as a local business the chance to boost your offline conversion, a chance that wasn't there even a year ago.

Here is an example of a local search for an automotive repair shop.

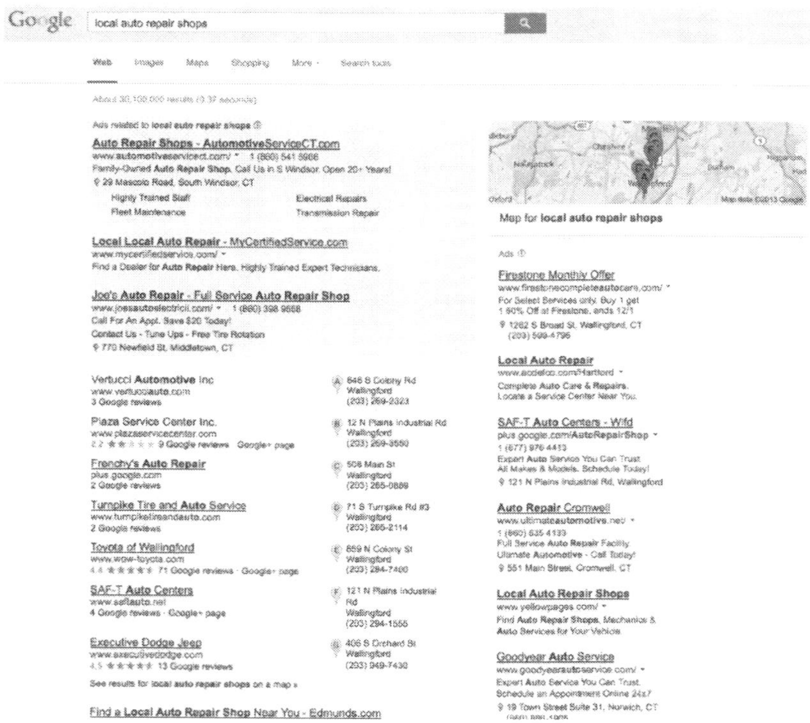

In the above figure you can see a big difference just by looking for a "local" auto repair shop, as opposed to finding "an" auto repair shop as in the figure on the next page. Google has done an extraordinary job with this, and every business should be part of this strategy.

Unfortunately, most aren't. It is increasing, but slowly. One other interesting thing that Google has done with their new service is this: You don't even need a website to rank on the first page of Google.

This reason alone is why anyone should get involved.

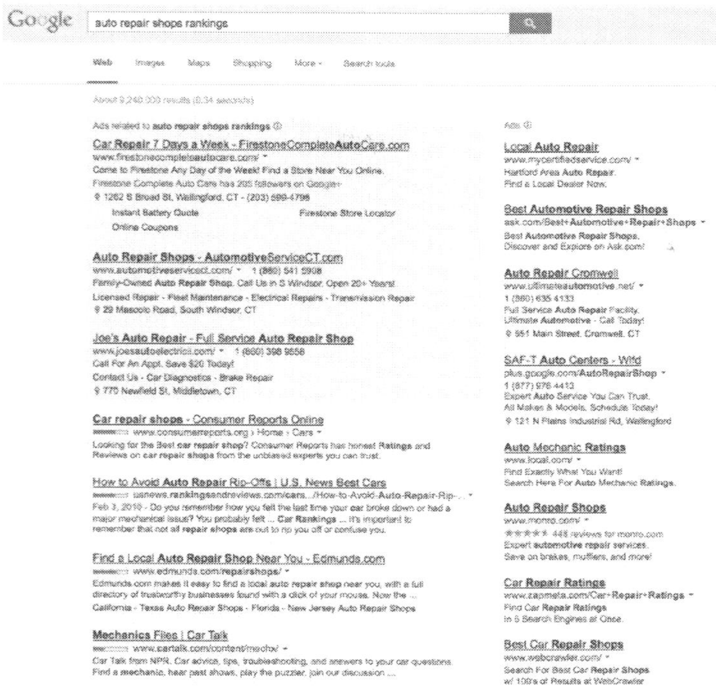

WARNING

We mentioned that Google has recently changed the way its search algorithms work (for trying to rank a website). One of these changes involves duplicate content. Now it's a bigger no-no than ever before.

Google has already said, many times, both verbally and in print, that it is now striving to reward real local businesses that have quality and substance to offer to their communities. As a result, they are cracking down even more harshly on anyone who's trying to game the system with shady methods of increasing their search ranking by adding duplicate content or fake listings. Such actions will now get you delisted from Google's search index entirely. Maybe even permanently.

Though this might seem harsh or unreasonable, remember: Google's efforts to clean up its search engine only benefits you. You want them to go after the scammers and spammers so that you, a real business who can offer value and quality to your local consumers, can rise to the top of their searches for people who are genuinely looking for help and services.

In a similar vein, be wary of companies who tell you the process of raising your search standing is easy. It's not. Some firms will tell you it's just a matter of keywords. Just buy content, they tell you, and put it on multiple sites and on your own.

The problem is that much of this content is almost always rehashed, rewritten or simply unoriginal, duplicated content. At best, you'll get next to no credit for it with Google, and at worst, you'll be delisted by them for it. .

This cuts two ways. Not only are you not gaining any ground, you're actually losing ground because Google's penalizing you. It's definitely not the way to go, and you'll be falling behind your competitors if you try and take this "easy" way out, no matter what an "expert" tells you about it.

Quality content has always been the centerpiece for being successful online, and that shows no signs of changing. Creating quality content doesn't have to be hard, but it does take time, patience and discipline. There's a process to follow to ensure that you have the right kind of quality content that will get you ranked sky-high on Google.

People have been trying to game the system with duplicate content and with link farms for years, but Google has caught on to this sort of trickery and it's rapidly disappearing from the search engine landscape. Make sure not to get scammed by any of these offers. You know that if it seems too easy or too inexpensive to be true, odds are that it probably is. Ask them if their content is duplicated or rewritten or if it appears anywhere else. If they hem and haw before answering, run for the hills and don't bother looking back.

But you probably haven't gone to those other companies. Instead, you bought this book. See. You are one step ahead of your competition already. With it, you've received the system and the process you need that will -- with some time, effort, patience and planning -- get you to the top of the search results for your area.

JUST THE FACTS:

- ✓ The Internet is no longer optional. More and more, people are using it to find businesses to fill their needs. You need to leverage that consumer activity.
- ✓ Search is the big player now in Internet marketing. You need to make sure your page ranks high in the list of results when users search.
- ✓ Be careful how you enter the search engine market. A substandard presence online can be worse than no presence at all
- ✓ If you need help, make sure to choose your marketers – and your "marketers" -- carefully. Some may attempt underhanded tricks to boost you in the search rankings (like duplicate content), but these tricks can often carry with them a severe penalty from the search engines for trying to game the system.
- ✓ Get onto Google places so you can get ranked more quickly.

Chapter 2

Pretty Websites Can Kill Your Business:

How to Get New Clients the RIGHT Way Online.

So now we know how important Google is. We've taken a look at how recent changes have made local search returns -- and Google rankings in general -- extremely important to your marketing efforts. We know that traditional media is fading fast, and if you want to stay on top of the game, you're going to have to get into this search business straight away.

The natural next step would be to go and get ranked, and for that it is best that you have your own website. An effective website is as much a part of this process as anything else, and if you're going to get good conversions from your search rankings, you need a functional website that fully caters to both the needs of your business and the needs of your customers.

In other words, don't do just a brochure type website.

The creation of the website can seem like a minefield, especially in today's whiz-bang, Flash-enabled, Web 2.0 world where everyone thinks every website needs interactive menus, drop-down interfaces, and all sorts of other bells and whistles. You see it all the time. People even ask for "Web 2.0" or "interactive" developers, and some developers push Flash this or Web 2.0 that on you, saying how important it is and how professional it makes your site look.

You may be tempted to believe them.

The truth, however, is this: for most small businesses and conversion rates, all of that fancy stuff does not matter. A solid, simple website will work far better at increasing your conversions and getting customers to contact you.

This may seem counter-intuitive -- especially in a world that seems to value style over substance -- but it's true: simpler pages have been far more effective at getting customers to call or email than other, fancier, flashier pages. That's true both in my experience and in the experience of others.

Creating a website may still seem a little daunting, especially considering how much we've been talking about the importance of getting listed properly. And that is true: getting ranked high on Google still matters the most. In fact, the rest of this book after this chapter is devoted to that very concept.

Your website, however, is an integral part of this whole chain. It's by no means the most important link in the chain, not by far, but it needs to be done well. If not, it could ruin the entire concept behind getting ranked on Google.

The bottom line is this: if your client doesn't actually pick up the phone and call, all that effort you put into getting visitors to your site will have been wasted. No matter how flashy, how fancy, how up-to-date your website is, if there are no conversions, then that website is not working for you, plain and simple.

So What Does A Good Website Look Like?

It's a good question and one not asked enough. If the flashy, stylish websites aren't for you, then what is? What is the secret to getting visitors to pick up the phone and call?

Let's take a look at the real scoop here and find out how to build the website that will get the most visitors who pick up that phone and call your office.

Site Construction: What Should Your Overall Site Look Like?

In general, there is a rule that can be applied to websites looking to garner conversions from local search returns: The less fancy the website is, the more conversions you'll get.

A solid, functional site will be far more effective for you. Keeping that in mind, here is a general outline of what a sample website layout might look like.

These are the basic pages you should have:

- Home page
- Blog
- About Us / Services
- Contact Us (with map and traceable phone number to call)

And that's it.

This might seem a bit *underwhelming* to you. We're talking about something vastly smaller than the majority of the websites you've visited. Those websites, however, are not yours.

(Note: The "Gallery Page" is where you might store pictures and video for use)

Your website is lean and mean. It's built for one purpose and one purpose only: to get people who go to your website to call you or email you.

You want someone who wants to *buy* something to contact you. Anything else is a waste. It's nice that people come to visit your site, maybe, but that doesn't mean anything if nobody calls you or if you don't capture someone's contact information (a phone number or email address) for future follow up.

Every page on your site should include a call to action. A call to action is something to get visitors to call you or email you right away. We'll talk more about the call to action later in the follow-up section.

Also, for local business websites I recommend, at a minimum, that you include a banner or header that appears on every page. Make sure your phone number appears in the top-right hand side or middle-right hand side of the page. Studies show, and my own experience confirms, that people's eyes gravitate toward the right side of a page. Look where Google puts their ads in their own search results. Right there.

For an added kick, add a form beneath the top phone number to sign up for your newsletter or to provide an incentive for people to provide you with their phone number or email address.

You are, of course, free to modify this layout however you wish. Depending on your business, you may want to add a page about upcoming events you are hosting, or about recent local news, or you might want to add a recent press release about your business. Do know, however, that this basic layout works extremely well, and always, always remember this: the less fancy the page, the better the results.

(Note: I use a website called www.hostednumbers.com to track all of my incoming phone calls and to track my marketing results so I know where my best marketing dollars are working for me – I will cover this more later on).

WARNING

Please do not confuse less fancy with bad design.

You still want your business and website to look professional, but I do advocate a clean simple design. In fact, I strongly feel that having less "flash" to a website often leads to a better visual design to start with. There is less clutter, and a clean visual design also helps with conversions. I'm talking the *feng shui* of web design.

Your business may already have invested in working with a branding agency to help create a logo and a set of colors that represent your "brand." It's important to carry those into your website to broadly reinforce your "brand." There are a number of color palette tools online where you can enter your businesses core colors and be given additional, visually appealing, complementary colors.

For example, Colour Lovers (http://www.colourlovers.com) or Color Combos (http://www.colorcombos.com).

Look, you are a valuable professional in your community and your services are not (and should not appear) cheap. Don't make your website give potential clients the wrong impression. You may not want to do it yourself, but that doesn't mean that you should hire your sister's friend's twenty-two year old kid who calls himself a webmaster, but lives in his parents' basement.

Your Website, Page by Page

Now let's break down each of these pages in-depth so we can understand them better.

The Home Page

Don't get too much "individuality" going on here. It is most important only that this page be easy on the eyes. It should have a blurb about you. It should invite the reader to explore more of the site. It should be easy to connect your reader with the rest of your site.

Your home page should have a USP (a Unique Selling proposition). A USP differentiates you from everyone else who does what you do. This is important. Your USP should be one of the first things the "clicker" should see when arriving at the site.

You also need to make absolutely sure that your home page features your blog prominently.

This is so important; I'm going to give the concept its own line:

Make sure the home page features your blog prominently.

There are many ways to do this. Some businesses have the actual blog on the homepage. If you prefer not to do this, think carefully about how to prominently integrate your blog with your home page.

Let me give you an example of why this is *so* important.

Let's say you're standing in front of a person and talking obsessively, never letting the other person speak, never allowing them to say a word. How would that other person feel? Better yet, what would they do?

They would get upset. They'd get angry if they could not participate in the conversation, right? I know I would. In fact, they would probably just walk away from you.

And they wouldn't want to talk to you again.

That is because communication is always a two way street. It is both give and receive. When both parties are talking about something they agree on, they will feel like continuing the conversation. They might even get to like each other more and might even get to better like what it is they're talking about.

Your marketing has to do the same. You cannot obsessively chatter to them (by constantly sending them mail or by having a one way, brochure type website). You need to give them a call to action, something they can do, or at least some way for them to communicate back.

Allowing the client or customer to get involved in a conversation about your product or service is *huge*. Now they can begin to like you better and be more interested in your product. They'll feel comfortable about buying the product or service you have available. They'll want to support you.

Blogs do this well. They allow the "other" part of the two-way communication to occur. They allow the recipient of your original communication to now get involved by interacting with you.

Get it?

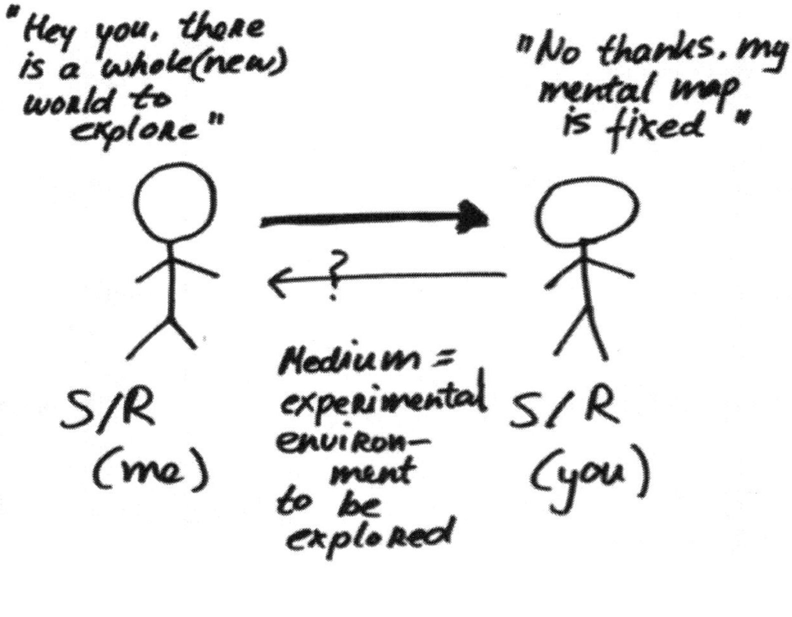

How about Video?

Video is another important component for your homepage. Studies have shown a thirty percent increase in conversions when a visitor can watch a video of someone from the business on the homepage. Yes, a thirty percent increase. Incorporate a small, short (90 second to 2 minute long) video somewhere on your home page.

I don't know about you, but I have noticed that today most folks read a lot less than they used to. This is why video is so important. It's a graphic way for you to portray yourself and to animate your USP. If it's short, its message will be grasped quickly and easily.

Okay. Now that you have gotten their interest, how do you keep them going?

Copy Is The Glue That Keeps 'Em There!

If you have any copy on your home page, make it about no more than these three things:

1. The benefits you provide someone. Not your services or your "features," but the actual benefits your clients will receive as a result of working with you. This is your USP explained as a benefit so it creates a customer's reach for the end result of the product or service you provide.
2. Information about what is on your blog and the links you list, which are enticements to view other good blog posts. I have also found that posting pictures or videos on blogs helps keep your viewers coming back
3. A call to action: what you can immediately provide to them in exchange for them calling you or providing you with their email or phone number. Special offers, special reports, checklists, etc. (Remember: always track how these offers succeed and where these prospects come from).

These three items are so important to the success of a website that I actually write these sections myself for my private clients and I place the copy word-for-word.

Your Blog

Don't underestimate the blog. It's one of the most vital (if not the most vital) parts of your website. It provides two components that are critical to your online success.

First, it is the home for new and relevant content for your prospects and clients. You can talk about an awful lot of things that will be relevant to them. You can discuss interesting things that are happening within the particular arena of business you're in and that immediately affect your readers. If you focus on auto repairs, for example, speak of the benefits of having a healthy automobile. You can also link to recent news articles and provide some of your own commentary about how they affect your readers.

A hidden gem of relevant content which most businesses overlook is talking about local news and information. It doesn't have to pertain directly to your business at all. You are a member of a community and if there is a big marathon, a 5k race, a festival or a parade coming up, then write a few paragraphs about it and include links so your viewers can get all the details in one place. If you know that parking is tough on Saturdays around that area, provide information about other parking. If there's a booth at the festival that's not to be missed, then tell your readers about that.

You might be surprised, but these blogs will become your most popular posts. They also build up your credibility as someone who lives in, works in and cares about your community.

You can also use books like *Who Knew?*, a book by Bruce Lubin and Jeanne Bossolina-Lubin giving 10,001 easy solutions to everyday problems.

Let me give you a few examples from it, which you could post:

For an automobile repair shop:

Keep Your Battery Clean So Your Car Starts Every Time

> To prevent your car's battery from corroding, wipe down the battery posts with petroleum jelly once every couple of months. Or let us know when getting your oil changed with us, and we will do it for no charge.

Or you could write something like this . . .

It's Time to Change Your Car's Air Filter

A clean air filter can improve your car's mileage by up to 10% (and at today's gas prices – that makes a difference in your monthly budget), so make sure yours is replaced regularly. Your car's filter should be changed at least every 8000 miles, but if you live in a sandy or highly polluted area, you should do it more often. A good rule of thumb is to simply have it changed every other oil change. This is something we check when you come to get an oil change here – we check it as part of our safety inspection.

Maybe you could write something like this . . .

Removing Bumper Stickers

We hate to break it to you, but John Kerry and John McCain lost their elections. Get those bumper stickers off and bring your car up to date (please)! Rub cold cream on the stickers and wait ten minutes. Then say goodbye to your former favorite candidates and peel the bumper stickers right off. Or, if you want, with your next visit, we will do it for you (no charge). So give us a call when you're ready ☺

See, it's real simple.

Of course, you can always find something to say about current affairs as well. The point is, just post. Be a part of your customer's life. Give them something they will enjoy. 10,001 solutions to everyday problems is a lot of stuff to write about. That one book can generate *lots* of helpful tips your customers will love.

The second thing a blog provides is a place for the search engines to find new and relevant content about what your business does and the location or locations where it provides those services. Everything we just discussed above helps accomplish that, and by talking about your industry or area, you will naturally use the keywords that search engines pick up. Furthermore, talking about things going on in the local community will help the search engines understand the community, the town and the city you need to be associated with in the search results.

Now that was all pretty simple, right?

Too often marketing agencies make this more complicated than it has to be. They talk about keywords, keyword density, latent search algorithms, and more. It doesn't have to be that hard.

Write about stuff you know and that provides value to your readers. The two most obvious topics are your area and the events going on in your community and nearby communities. If you hear someone talking about keyword density, just run away, as with that obsessive talker. In my humble opinion, they're just trying to make it sound that complicated so they can charge you more.

Over the years, I have learned a lot working in particular with auto repair shops. While I know that consistent blogging is important, getting my clients to actually write twice a week, in addition to the daily tasks they have to do, was sometimes like trying to saddle a cow. That's why I recently made the decision to convince my clients to hire staff writers (good ones who actually know how to write, not graduate students who spit out abstract, academic gibberish) and pay them well. The results are worth it. My clients get good content several times per week, which brings in more customers…and they don't have to do any of the work.

That's how important blogging is to me.

Here is a good example (figure on next page):

What Do My Vehicle Warning Lights Mean?

Posted: October 30, 2013

Nothing is more frustrating than when a vehicle warning light comes on and you don't know what it means. To help you better identify theses dashboard warning symbols, we crafted this vehicle warning light guide. Our goal at Christian Brothers Automotive is to educate our customers so they feel safe on the road. Read More

4 Important Winter Automotive Maintenance Tips

Posted: September 30, 2013

As winter quickly approaches, it's important to perform simple preventative maintenance steps to stay safe in the blustery conditions. Investing in these simple repairs could be the difference in arriving to your destination on time or waiting for a tow truck on the side of the road. Read More

Reward a Teacher Who Has Made a Difference

Posted: September 10, 2013

How can you give an Apple to your favorite teacher? Tell us how they've made a difference in your community, and your favorite teacher could win a brand new Apple iPad Mini plus gift cards for school supplies and free auto care. Plus the grand prize is a pizza party for the entire school! Read More

Tire Safety and Maintenance

Posted: July 24, 2013

The four tires on your vehicle are the only things separating you from the road. Are you giving them as much attention as they warrant? Proper tire inflation, tread depth, alignment and rotation can add up to a safer, more cost-efficient ride.

Tire Tread Depth Read More

What is a Slipping Transmission and Is It Serious?

Posted: June 6, 2013

A slipping and irregular transmission can signal major problems in your vehicle's transmission, which can result in costly transmission repairs. Oftentimes, low transmission fluid levels or the wrong viscosity (thickness) of transmission fluid can cause your transmission to slip and function improperly.

Read More

The "About Us" Page

The "About Us" page is, oddly enough, one that many businesses get wrong. They're all too content just to throw up a little blurb about themselves, or about the partners, with perhaps a map or two on how to get to them. This isn't enough info on you, nor is it helping you drive conversions.

People care about your years of experience as a business owner (or how you can help them), sure, but that's not what's going to get them to call. It doesn't truly distinguish you from the others in your line of work, or give them a reason to give you their business. You have to think instead about the *unique selling position* we spoke of earlier and why clients do like to work with you and continue working with you. Information about you, your business, why you're different, etc. – you have to show them why you're ahead of the pack, and ultimately show them why they, as a consumer, want to work with you and not the other guy.

Think about it this way: most people care about one thing and one thing only and are tuned into their own special radio station, "WIIFM." That stands for "What's in It for Me." Your prospects could honestly care less about your degrees, titles, or positions. Sorry! What they really want to know is if you can solve their problem, and solve it fast and professionally while being pleasant to them.

So instead of talking about you, talk about them and what they will benefit from working with you.

That one tip alone, in fact, will set your website above and beyond most of the small businesses I see and even some I work with: they simply don't set themselves apart sufficiently. By doing so, you'll gain a very competitive edge in your industry.

The "Contact Us" Page

The "Contact Us" page should be simple. You should have your email, your phone number, and a map to your business. That's it.

You can perhaps put a slightly different or stronger call to action on this page, but for the most part this page should be clean and simple and have nothing to distract the reader from picking up the phone or entering their email.

Some people do add a contact form on this page. That's perfectly fine to do, but the most important thing is to provide a clear phone number or an email address for your viewers, which is directed and answered by an actual human.

In some industries you will want to have an appointment section instead of a "Contact Us" link. In other words, you want the website to convert, right?

So now you've got the basic layout of your page. Just one thing left to do: Make your call to action work for you. Without being "salesy."

As I said earlier, you should first of all have a phone number from www.hostednumbers.com just for this website. And if you have a blog, it should have a completely separate phone number on it so you can track which number is producing more results.

Yes, I am saying that *every* single marketing piece should have its own phone number so you can track it individually. Plus, Hosted Numbers captures the caller ID. So, if you missed a call, you can redial them back. Or, in some cases, it can capture a list of these phone numbers and later on you can do a "phone blast" (blasting a recorded message to everyone at once).

Okay, now that I got that out of my system, let's go back to the contact or appointment. Bottom line, the faster you can solve your prospect's problem, the faster they convert to a customer.

Then you have a chance to gain a client (not a customer).

Let me explain. A "customer" to me is like a "one night stand." A "customer" came in for the "cheap" introductory offer. He did not up-sell or come back in for another service.

When this happens, I hear my own clients say things like "Groupon" did not work. Well, it did work. The customer was there, right? What did not work was the next step: turning the "customer" into a "client."

A "client" to me is a customer who you build a relationship with. Someone who returns to your establishment – many times – if handled correctly – and refers you to his or her family and friends. This person is much like the fan of a sports team. That team can get beat to death in a game, yet the fans still defend the team. This is a true "client," as far as I am concerned. He is more than a "one night stand."

So a good call to action is *vital* to all marketing, as I explained before. Here is what an effective call to action could look like on an auto repair shop website:

Here are a couple of examples of fantastic call to actions:

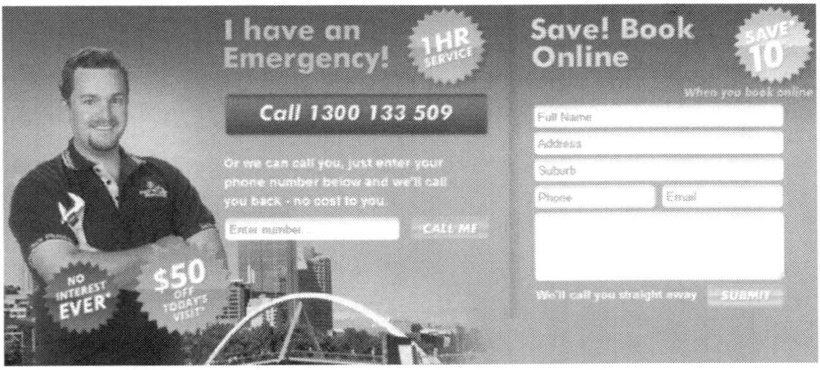

Notice the call to action is plain and simple. And it's easy to find. It's clear what you want the prospect to do. And, the phone number or contact information is on the upper right corner like we spoke of earlier.

A “call to action” is the command for what you want the prospect to do so it must be *simple, simple, simple.*

If not, the prospect gets lost and never gets his problem solved by you, but by someone else.

By the way, many times I have had a client who at first glance had what looked like a fantastic ad, only to then find there was no real call to action. The business owner would be insisting marketing (or the Internet) didn’t work.

What didn’t work was what wasn’t there. A call to action.

So what makes an effective call to action, and how can you put that to use on your website to generate those conversions?

An effective call to action is one that makes the customer pick up the phone and call right away or give you their email. In other words, he or she gives you a way to continue communication. It’s crucial that your call to action be strong because you’re asking for information that’s become more and more private in today’s world. People know about spam, they know about scams, and they’re hesitant to give out their email to just any site they find on the Internet.

You have to overcome that initial hesitation and get them to give you their email or to call you.

One way is to offer a special – like a big discount on a service – for providing information or for calling now.

I’ve found the way that works best, however, is to provide a special report about something that will be helpful to the consumer who found you by searching for your type of product or service in your local area. Examples of this could be:

- “Special Report: 3 critical things you need to know before ever hiring or calling an ____________(insert target niche / business type here)”

- “5 things you need to know before hiring an ____________(insert target niche / business type here) “

- “3 myths you’ve been led to believe about ____________.”

It's important that these examples be specific to your business. The more targeted your examples, the more likely you're going to get someone to sign up who's interested in your area of practice. You can make it even more targeted by making it local, for example "3 things you need to know before hiring a ______ in Little Rock, Arkansas."

These examples should be strong enough to get someone to put in their email or to call you. The viewer should say, "Hey, wow, what are those three things? I was ready to get moving and hire a ___________ (blank) tomorrow, but I better know this before I do anything." Then they pop in their email and you can quickly follow up with them. You can even automate some of the follow-up.

This content is so important that for my private clients, I write the report for them and place it on their website (after their review, of course). The titles above take a "consumer advocacy" approach. I've found this gets a lot more clients than most of today's traditional advertising.

I also typically recommend that you not just ask for their email, but for their cell phone number as well. People are giving out their cell phone numbers more readily now, much more so than a few years ago, where it was very difficult to get someone's mobile number. Many people nowadays use cell phones as their primary or even only phone number, and thus they're more willing to give it out to people who ask for it – if the reason is compelling enough

That's the key: giving them a compelling enough reason to overcome the concern for privacy I mentioned earlier. These "special reports" can do that.

If you follow all these steps, anyone who enters their email or phone number will be a "warm" lead. A "warm" lead is someone who's going to be receptive to your business and who's going to be much easier to convert into a client because they've already shown a great deal of interest in your services. In fact, they've pretty much done what for you is the hard part, getting in contact. You have to act on this, however. Warm leads, like anything else that's warm, tend to cool over time. If you don't act quickly, it'll be that much harder to seal the deal.

This leads us to our next item of interest: follow-up systems.

It's important that you have some sort of follow-up system in place so that you can call a lead within five minutes after they've entered their email or phone number into an online form. After all, most people want instant gratification and solutions. It's vital that you have a stable, reliable follow-up system in place.

Get back to them within five minutes. You know they're an extremely warm lead. You know they were on the website, you know they were interested, and you know they're looking for business. This is a much warmer lead than someone who just happened to see your name in a direct mail piece or in a local flyer.

There are some automated follow-up systems that are used by many businesses, tools like Instant Customer – which fully integrates with Constant Contact – and Infusionsoft, among others. Depending on your business, there are even some services that provide dozens of pre-written email templates that have proven to help convert email prospects into clients. If you want to use these, that's perfectly fine, but make sure to put the call to action form on that all-important right-hand side first.

We'll talk more about follow-up later in its own in-depth, complete section.

First, however, let's get to the real deal, the heart and soul of this book. Before you launch that website, let's talk about building it to make sure it gets noticed and gets found by the search engines that send people to your site.

JUST THE FACTS:

- ✓ Don't lose focus when designing a website: a website is for one purpose and one purpose only, and that's to get people to get in touch with you.
- ✓ Fancy is never better: plain is best here. Avoid whiz-bang, Flash sites. Get a good designer to make a clean, simple, functional web site that converts leads.
- ✓ Blogs are a vital part of a website's success. Put yours on your home page, or at least feature your blog prominently on your home page.
- ✓ Following up quickly on potential clients is absolutely critical. You should have automated systems in place that follow-up with your customers the moment they get in touch with you.

Chapter 3

Words, Words, Words: How to Choose the Right Keywords to Promote Your Business

Having a website is all well and good, but it doesn't do much for you when nobody visits it.

We're going to get Google to notice you and rank you highly, and we'll do this by using targeted keywords. I'm not going to make this as complicated a discussion as some of those other "experts" do, but keywords are an important concept for you to understand.

What are they? Keywords are the words (either one word or multiple words) that users type into Google (or other search engines like Yahoo, etc.) before they click "Search." A multiple-word keyword, like "oil change on my Mercedes," (in the auto repair business) is called a "long-tail keyword phrase." When a user enters one of these keyword phrases, they will get back what Google thinks is most relevant response to their search. More specifically, Google returns what it thinks are the best websites offering the product or service for the specific keyword phrase that the user has entered into the search box.

That, in a nutshell, is what a keyword is and what it does.

Our questions, however, are going to be a tad more complicated: What keywords should we use? What keywords will get Google to notice that we're the best search result for a specific keyword phrase?

Many businesses have chosen me and my staff to do their Internet marketing for them, but when I first sit down at the table with them to discuss plans for their Internet marketing strategies, I see two mistakes they make almost every time we start talking about keywords.

A new client will be excited to show me that they have the number one alphabetical ranking for their particular business, like "ABC Auto Repair." They're so excited, in fact, that it's almost tough to tell them that that's nothing to be excited about. Almost no one is searching for their exact company name on the Internet.

If they are, it means they already know the company and know what the company does. They've probably been reached already by one of the company's other marketing techniques. You no longer need to be wasting any time trying to find them. Besides, Google and the other search engines already do a pretty good job of making sure that your website is going to rank high with your business name alone for any people who search within twenty-five miles of your location.

Never forget: you're using the Internet to get new customers who are trying to solve a problem that you and your business can solve. In short, you need to present an attractive solution to the problem these people have.

In the auto industry, for example, people need help with "oil change, quick." "long-term auto care," "European auto repair," or drivability issues like "check engine light is on." These are the keywords people are putting into the search box. Nobody's looking for "Jones, Smith, and Johnson, LLC." They're looking for "oil change, quick," "long-term auto care," "European auto repair." They're typing in specific problems that an auto mechanic can provide a solution for.

You want to rank yourself by these keywords, not by your business name, clever and dear to your heart as that business name might be.

The second big mistake I see made all the time is businesses trying to rank themselves in terms that only make sense to someone who works in that particular industry.

For example, again in the auto industry – where I have many clients – one I've seen frequently is the keyword phrase "tune up." Not many people know that "tune up" is an entire part of the auto industry, and although they might learn about this term and then start searching for it in the future, they're not doing so in great numbers right now. What the ideal tune up prospect is typing in is "my engine light is on," "check engine light," or even "engine light." People may or may not understand the terminology "Tune Up," but they do know what they're really looking for is someone to help them with their check engine light.

Google actually provides data about what terms people are searching with and while it sometimes requires a little thought to interpret the date, Google provides it for free.

The most important thing to remember in keyword selection is this: you must look at keywords from the user's perspective. You can't expect them to search for the terms you believe they're going to be able to define. Use that free Google service.

Don't ever go to your industry association definitions for keywords – unless, of course, it's to see which keywords not to use. It's a trap that many people often fall into, and you've got to watch out for it.

Even I'm not immune to it. I deal heavily in search and social media Internet marketing, and when I'm not careful, sometimes I find myself using terms people wouldn't use and don't care about: "SEO," for instance, or "social media measurement." These are terms my clients would never type in. If they were looking for a marketing consultant, maybe they would type in something like "I want to get more customers." Those are the keywords I really care about.

These are the two big pitfalls I see with most businesses that I work with, and they both stem from one thing: a lack of knowledge. Specifically, the knowledge of what people are searching for. There are a number of tools that exist out there in addition to the free Google service, but they do change more frequently than I can list here.

Clients who know how to use them will benefit from the services they provide.

The best and fastest way, however, to find the right keywords is just to ask your family and friends. Think back to the first chapter where we said that it's ordinary people who are using Google to search with. That's also true for keyword use.

Ask your friends, your colleagues and your neighbors for help. What would they type in? Ask someone you know to explain to someone else what you do and listen to what they say. They'll use plain English terms to describe your business, and those are the terms that ordinary people are going to type into that search box.

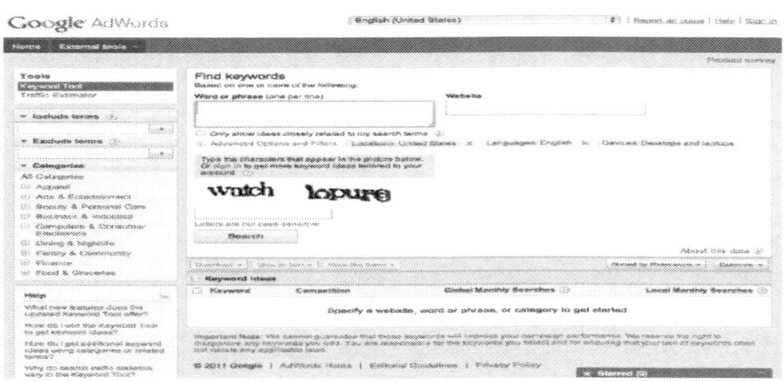

You can find the above (in the image) Google tool by typing into a search engine (like Google.com) the words: "key word tool."

Or you can use this paid tool that I've located:
http://www.keyworddiscovery.com

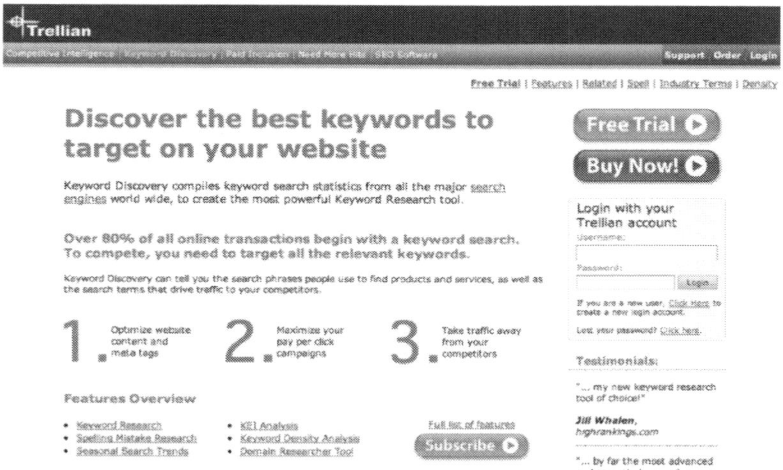

Go here to find this tool: http://www.keyworddiscovery.com

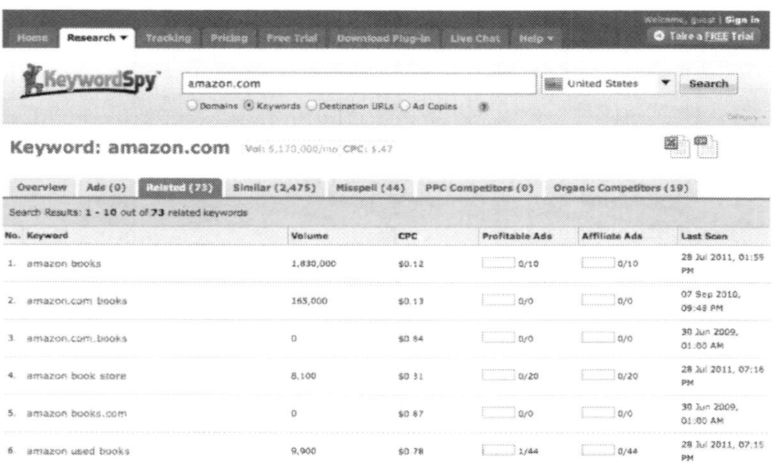

Here's another paid tool that is a spy on your competition:
http://www.keywordspy.com

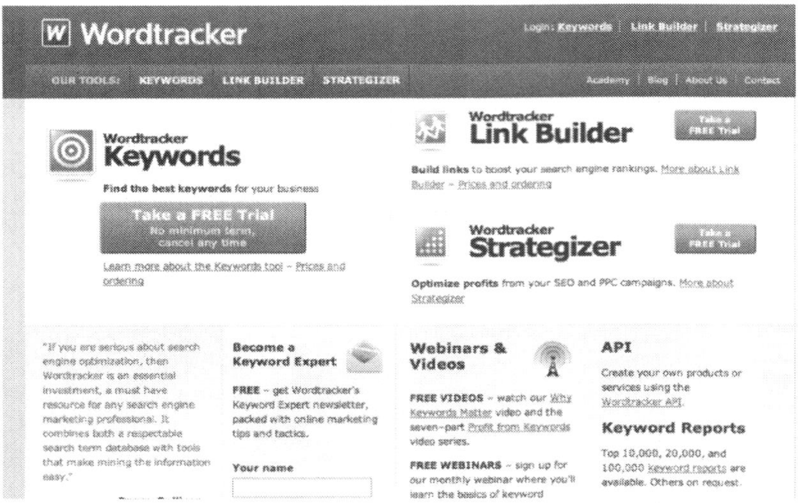

Here's a reliable tool for back links and key words: http://www.wordtracker.com

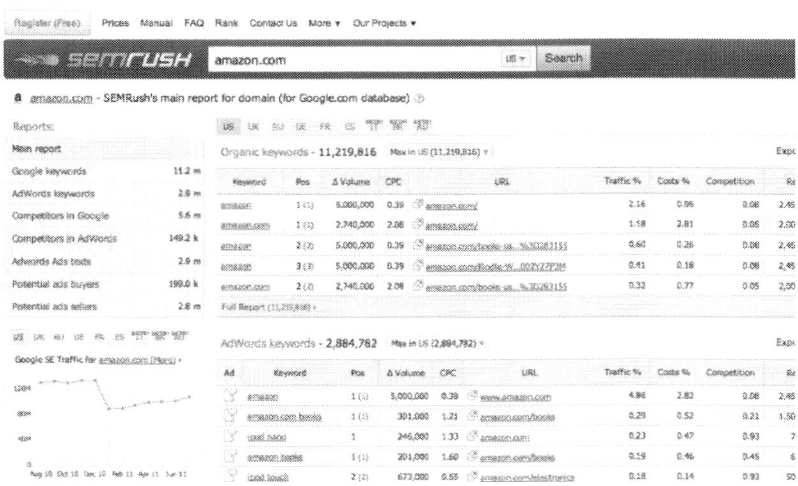

Last but not least, go here for statistics: http://www.semrush.com

Another way I gather good key words is to survey past invoices. In other words, go back through at least three months of past sales invoices. Tally up each service sold. You'll see some services sell more than others. Once you have located the services or products that sold the most, see what problems those products or services solved. You'll start to notice that the same words or phrases keep popping up.

Now you have something to put into Google's search engine keyword tools, and it works well.

It works because you've gotten into the mind of a client. If *you* gave a sixty second description of what you do for a client, and then they turned around and tried to tell that to a friend, it's not going to sound the same. In fact, odds are it'll be very different indeed.

What you're looking for, therefore, in keyword selection is not how you describe your business. It's how your clients and prospects describe it. If you're not using the keywords that these people are searching for, you're not going to rank high enough for anyone to find you.

All this might be a little overwhelming. Don't worry. I'm not saying you have to nail this on the first try. You can always change your keywords over time. It's not the end of the world if you choose the wrong keyword on Day 1. Keywords can be modified, refined, or even completely switched out altogether. And they often are, as you fine-tune your search results.

Also, don't over-think your keyword selection to the point that you freeze up. Start off by asking your neighbors and friends, as we described above. This is the best method for finding keywords initially. As you get more advanced, you can start using some of the tools we talked about above to refine your keyword selection. Those tools will definitely benefit you in the long run, but they're not crucial right out of the gate.

Just start simply, as described above, and slowly grow in complexity as you master each step of the process.

One way to refine keyword selection even further is to use Google's "Related Searches" tool. This will give you an idea of what others are searching for when they search for your keywords and may give you an insight into related terms that you may not have thought of before.

Another important tool in your keyword research arsenal is the Google Keyword Tool (GKT, for short). GKT is important because although the Related Searches tool gives you suggestions, GKT gives you returns for how many people per month are actually searching for that keyword. This is across the entire US, so you're going to have to make an educated (and usually valid) assumption that those will also work in your locality the same as they work nationally.

Here's how this works. Let's stick with our earlier example. We'll type in the two terms "tune up" and "check engine light."

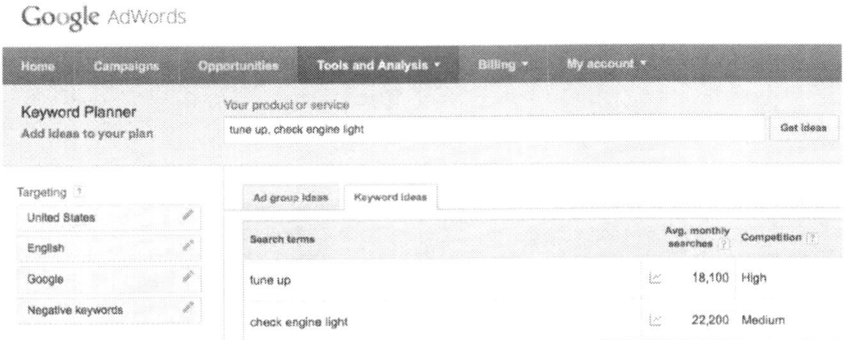

You'll notice in the screenshot above that "check engine light" gets more hits than "tune up." You see, "tune up" is not the problem. It's the solution. You might not even want to target "tune up" initially. It could even bring in the wrong customer, one who might not be happy to find out you don't provide the real solution to the actual problem he's having, but couldn't pinpoint with his search.

I've found that you can assume that these national numbers will apply reasonably well to local searches. It's not a one hundred percent given, of course, but there's no effective tool out there right now for pinpointing exact numbers of local searches, so use this one.

If you really want a good idea of how many local searches those national numbers signify, by the way, you can make this rough calculation. Take the last census data for the total US population and take the census of your location. Divide your location by the total population and you'll get a rough estimate of your percentage of the total population. Multiply that times the keywords to get the number of local searches with that keyword.

For example, let's say you live in a city with one million people. The US has 300 million, by last count, which means your city has 1/300th of the overall population's number of searches. "Check engine light" returns 300k hits per month, so we can assume that your locale is getting about 1000 searches per month on that keyword. It's not exact, but it's a good "guesstimate" and is often more spot-on than you'd expect.

By the way, do not think that bigger is always better. Sometimes, it's better to go after an "easily-dominated" keyword, and I'll show you how to do that in the discussion that follows on niche marketing.

The other pitfall that companies make is they typically want a neat, catchy name or their business name in the URL (Uniform Resource Locator: your website's "address"). If you want to rank well, though, you're going to have to make your URL keyword rich.

Here's an example: Let's say you're the Johnson and Smith Auto Repair shop in Dallas, Texas, and you've decided on the keyword phrase "Auto Repair Dallas TX." A great URL for your website, then, would be "http://www.AutoRepairDallasTX.com." That's going to help tremendously in your efforts to rank high on Google.

I realize that's not a pretty name, but if you want to have your business name and your website URL for business cards and marketing materials, you still can. It's both cheap and easy to have multiple domain names. You can then have your webmaster redirect traffic from "http://www.johnsonandsmithautorepair.com" to "http://www.AutoRepairDallasTX.com" and still reap the benefits of the keyword-rich URL while having your "professional" URL on your business cards.

A keyword-rich URL is the first thing you can do to influence your Google search rankings. We'll talk about other methods to rocket you to the top, of course, but if you start this process without a keyword-rich URL, it's going to be a steep uphill battle. Do yourself a favor then and get a keyword-rich URL. It'll make everything down the line much, much easier.

Why "niching" or niche marketing works so well

Here's another facet of Internet marketing that you do need to know about: "niching." As you may have guessed, even with a keyword-rich URL, you can't be highly ranked in everything. Your URL, no matter what it is, will always be too specific. Unless you're the only business like yours in a small town – or perhaps a general business – there's going to be a ton of other businesses like yours vying for that top spot through many different keywords.

So you're going to want to select some specialty or niche to focus on.

This isn't to say that you can't do other things or cross-sell once you get your client, but you definitely have to step back and create a business strategy for niching.

Where does most of your revenue come from? You probably noticed this when you did those surveys from your invoices. What's your most profitable product or service of the business? Some of these require a significant amount of time from you, while there are others that can be done with your staff actually doing most of the work. The second is often the more profitable.

Next you need to decide what niche you want to emphasize with keywords.

What it comes down to is this: to dominate online, you have to know where you want to go and focus on that one thing. Find something that you'd be happy with if ninety-five percent of your business came from that one thing. Perhaps it's the product or service that you've found is most wanted by your customers. It's there and waiting for you, and now you're going to want to start with it in regards to your keywords.

Dominating the search rankings under the correct key words or long tail key words all at once is going to be hard, if not outright impossible. Start with the most important product or service of your business, and the one you now most want to go after. The most profitable to you may not be where you started, but it has to be where you want to go, the niche that you want to dominate in the future.

Dominating that one keyword phrase means owning that particular source of business in your town.

In keeping with our tune up example, let's say you want to dominate the keyword "check engine light." You'd make a keyword-rich URL out of that keyword-rich phrase, and then proceed to dominate the search rankings with your carefully crafted process, now honed razor-sharp to focus on that particular niche.

Once you've narrowed down between three and five keyword phrases, with just a few words in each, you'll want to make sure those keyword phrases are in your "title tag," which are the first few sentences of the copy in your website. That title tag should *always* start with those keywords. You want the title tag to start with those keywords, then name your business location, and end with your business name. This feeds the search engines the right information in the right sequence to boost your ranking.

Don't lead with your business name. Here, your business name can just come along for the ride. It's already all over your website, and people (and Google) aren't going to miss it. Start instead with your most important keywords, and make sure those are peppered all throughout your site.

WARNING

Don't overdo it, though.

Google is looking for real people with real content, not automatons who simply spew out keywords nonstop.

There's a joke in the Search Engine Optimization world about this:

Q: How many Search Engine experts does it take to change a light bulb?

A: Light. Bulb. Lamp. Fluorescent. Incandescent. LED. Flashlight…

The joke is light-hearted, but the message is clear: don't over-saturate. Make sure your keywords hover around four percent density in the page text. This is the optimal ratio of keywords to words.

Okay, I said I wouldn't try to confuse you with terms like "keyword density" and here I've gone and just brought it up. I apologize, although you now know the specific data if you choose to use it, and obviously I thought it was important enough to risk a little contradiction of my earlier comment.

Another important thing to consider in this strategy is whether or not you're in an area where someone else is already dominating that larger keyword phrase. If someone's dominating the keyword phrase you want, you have to focus on smaller subsets of that keyword phrase. In other words, if you can dominate two or three smaller keyword phrases, you may actually end up getting more business than the company that just went after only the larger, broader term.

These last two strategies are the ones you have to look at from an insider's perspective. They are important for a business owner to understand to be successful.

They make you more knowledgeable. They enable you to do it yourself, or to be fully savvy when you hire a business to do it for you. If you do hire an outside business, you'll be able to make sure it's not just some webmaster who puts up a quick website. Instead, you want someone who will ask these tough questions and really help you to think through the right online strategy for you.

Just like the duplicate content folks we mentioned in Chapter One, there are lots of people just trying to sell you something quick, down and dirty instead of doing things the right way. Don't get fooled. Never go into any negotiations without knowing beforehand what your marketing business should provide you.

Once you've got your keywords, your domain name, and your website ready, it's time to step up your game. To do this we're going to get into blogging to help your ranking, and we're going to take a look at some more advanced, but simple local search techniques as well.

JUST THE FACTS:

- ✓ Keywords are important. Don't bother trying to rank for your business name. Rank with keywords that get traffic and are terms that ordinary users are searching for.
- ✓ Incorporate your keywords into your website and have a webmaster forward your professional-looking URL to your keyword rich one.
- ✓ Specialize, specialize, specialize. Don't go for the broad market. Find your niche or specialty and aim towards that.
- ✓ Leverage your marketing tools. Get help from the people right around you. They are, for the most part, representative of your clients and can offer insight into how your clients would search for you.
- ✓ Be natural. Google and Bing don't like keyword stuffing. Don't ever go over four percent keyword density. For your text, if you just write naturally, you'll almost always you'll have a good amount of keyword density and a natural, easy-to-read flow to your copy.

Chapter 4

Let's Get Local: Blogging and Advanced Local Search Techniques

If you've been following this guide thus far, you've got a reasonable website setup going. In fact, you're probably better off than anybody who just threw up a website to have an Internet presence, and you're definitely better off than anyone who has refused the transition to web-based marketing.

You may even have pulled a lead or two just from having the website, and you're considering putting your Google Places / Google + Local page up right away so you can watch your website skyrocket to the top of those local search returns.

I like your style, but hold on to your seat. Your site's still small-fry.

In this chapter, we're going to figure out how to make your local business big-fry on the web by using some more advanced local search techniques.

Blogging

Google has emphatically said that they're going to give stronger credit to resources that are both relevant to the user and current. This makes sense, given the overall makeup of the Internet. Content ages quickly, and newer info is often far more useful to a person searching than old info. This problem is usually dealt with by adding new content to static web pages, but this method is so time-consuming, it's more trouble than it's worth.

The solution? Blogging.

It is true that blogging has become the online activity-du-jour on the Internet. It seems that everyone and their cat has one, and sometimes several. The fact of the matter is, however, that blogging has become a powerful force on the Internet. It also has the one distinct advantage that it's by far the easiest, most convenient, and most effective way to add new, updated content to your website.

You don't have to go in and change copy all the time, you don't have to deal with static pages, HTML, and minor edits, you just have to update your blog every now and then.

It's especially helpful when you consider Google's other preference in high-ranking Google search results: steady, relevant content. There's no "magic bullet" or fast-track way to get to the top of the Google search rankings, and in this case, slow and steady wins the race. Blogging is absolutely, positively one hundred percent all about this. It's essentially the vehicle that allows you to easily make regular, useful updates to keep your site both relevant and full of a steady stream of new content.

To that end, there's a minimum amount of blog posts you should be putting out each week. Because of Google's preference for updated, steady content, you should be blogging at the very least once per week, and each blog post should be between 250 and 800 words. Blogs can be longer, but they don't need to be, but they definitely shouldn't be any shorter than 250 words or Google may mark them down as non-useful.

Writing a blog may seem daunting to many, and understandably so. The thought of composing one more written piece each week isn't appealing to most folks out there. If you think about it, though, once a week isn't too bad. Really, that's only four times a month. If you make a schedule and stick to it, you'll find that blogging isn't the chore you first thought it would be.

If, after you've been doing it for a while, you find that you have time for more, go for it. It's beneficial to put up two new blog posts each week. That's the optimum number, and two blogs per week will net you the most positive credit when Google compiles its local search returns.

Twice a week, however, is plenty. Don't go over that. Some people come into this with a slightly linear mindset. They think that since two is better than one, five must be better than two. It's not. You'll experience a diminished rate of return in this regard. Two blog posts a week is much better than one, but five blog posts a week is barely better than two. If you're blogging more than two times a week, stop. There are other, better things you could be doing with your time.

Blog subjects

Having a blog is all well and good, but a blog without useful, relevant content is hardly a blog at all. To that end, you're going to need to fill your blog with useful, quality content that maximizes the amount of utility that Google perceives in your site. Here are the three main content points you should be hitting in your blog posts:

3) Talk about what you do

This one may seem pretty obvious, but it's worth mentioning. Talk about what you do, not who you are. Don't talk about yourself, how long your business has been around, how great your service is. That isn't going to help you any. You need to fill your blog posts with quality content that relates to the services you do. Google sees quality content as what's valuable or useful to the user.

For example, let's say you're an auto mechanic. You could talk about getting emissions or inspections done or about what to do in different weather conditions as preventative actions for a car. A perfect blog post about seasonal tips for a car would cover these changes or provide the relevant information about them.

You could title one "7 Things You Need to Know about Your Car before the Winter to Prevent Break Downs" and write it as an easygoing, inside look at how your clients could do it themselves, but let your readers know that your shop makes it easy to do and what means for them.

2) Plugged in: Talk about local events

The first tip on this list might seem obvious to most, but this trick isn't. And, of all of them, this is the *super-ninja* secret of Internet marketing. Talk about local events. Blogging about local goings on and tying them back into what you do is a great, great way to make Google take notice and gain credit in the local search return results.

For example, if you live in a city and there's a big event coming up, talk about the big event and how it relates to your community. Or let's say you live in a college town and every Saturday during football season the town quadruples in size. Sometimes these events polarize a college town. Some local residents are proud of their team; some are frustrated by the commotion of the big event. Some think it's good for business, some think it's bad.

You can offer suggestions for parking those Saturdays or list some must hit restaurants after the game or just throw out some other local activities for those who want to avoid the game and the increased traffic. Don't get caught up in the polarization, but write a blog that's helpful to both sides.

These blogs in particular help you with Google because Google will see that you're a part of the community and, more importantly, your blog posts give Google lots of keyword clues about your location, and these help you rise to the top of the rankings in your location.

Don't get tangled up in local legal issues in your community. Shy away from them, no matter how much a current topic of interest they are. Everyone has a political opinion and you don't want to seem to favor one side or the other.

Overall, though, these local community posts are as valuable in their own way as any other blogs you might make elsewhere. Someone who searches you will have plenty of time browsing your site and blogs to see your other posts and find out about what you do and how you do it. These also help your business come out on top in the location it's in because of the connection and keyword clues mentioned above.

If, for instance, someone searches for "auto repair dallas tx," you'll show up because of both your blog posts and your location-based (Dallas, TX), community-based blog posts. Too many businesses don't do this, which is understandable because, on the surface, it doesn't make sense to talk about things that aren't related to what you do.

But that was before the Internet, before Google and before search engine ranking strategies.

TIP:

You can always refer to yourself with your keywords. Don't overdo it, but it's perfectly fine to write things like "As an auto repair shop in Dallas, Texas, I'm always surprised when..." That will give you the best of both worlds.

Another great proactive tip is to go to the local newspaper site, see what they're covering, and link back to the newspaper site while you write about it on your blog yourself. It's easy research.

I personally use PLR's (Public Label Rights). That means you buy the rights to an article and because you own the article, you can change it however you like. It's not perjury. This helps you to have hundreds of articles to articulate at any time. In fact, I have often ranked a website well within the first ninety days by blogging once a day for those ninety days and in those same ninety days submitting articles simultaneously.

Here are a few websites to make this simple:

For the content go to: http://bigcontentsearch.com

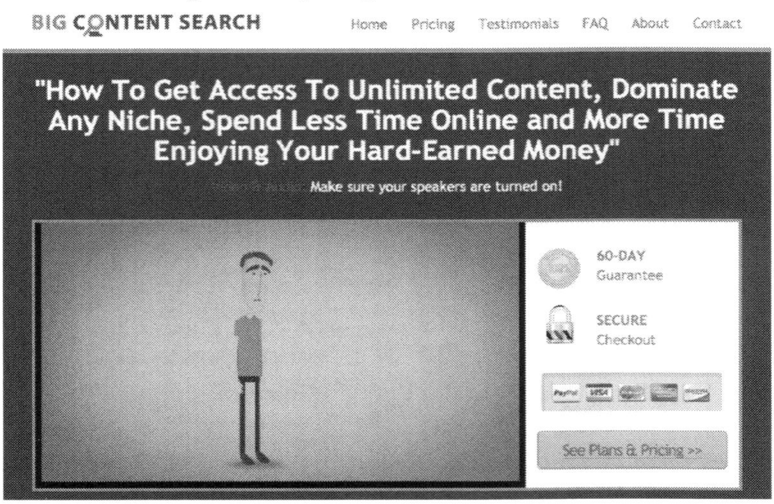

For article submission to over 800 sites at once, go to: http://www.spindistribute.com

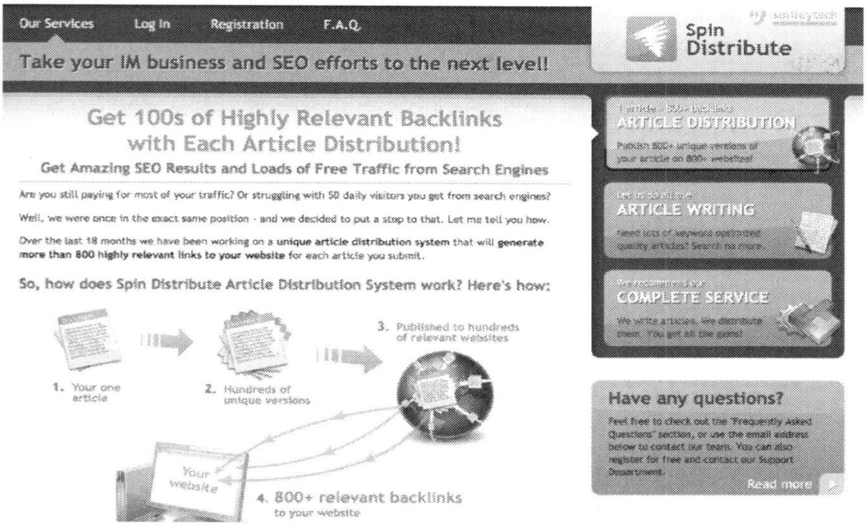

To turn your blog into a PDF, go here: http://www.zinepal.com

To submit the PDF, go to: http://www.slideshare.net, http://www.docstoc.com, https://app.box.com, http://www.scribd.com, or http://en.gravatar.com

By submitting your articles to these links, you won't have to rely on just SEO. If Google changes their algorithm, you will have these sites sending you "backlinks" (clicks from other sites to yours) regardless of the latest fade with Google (or others like it).

Google loves this "link juice." It makes Google feel like you are terribly popular and they'll rank you better for it.

These blogs also have the added advantage of making you seem more likeable and down-to-earth to the public, too, which always pays a huge bonus in client interaction. When someone finds your blog and reads through it, it'll be enjoyable. They'll not only just be getting practical auto advice; they'll also begin to feel some connection to you as well. When they read your blog, they won't be seeing just another faceless auto technician (or whatever work you are in). They'll read your blog posts about the community and think "Gee, this person has a personality. They know what they're talking about. They are a part of my community and they're invested in it."

That person is more likely to pick up the phone and give you a call, right?

You just got a warm lead simply by being a personable blogger who talks about the local community.

3) Be natural

This ties into the last point as well. Be natural.

You don't always have to sound like the smartest person in the world on your blog. This isn't to say you should be sloppy or stupid, but you shouldn't sound like a king preaching from atop the ivory tower either. Your clients (and Google) like to see content and blog posts that appear to be and actually are from normal people. Conversation, stories and anecdotes are all things they like to index. Conversing on your blog makes you more reachable and more indexable (ranked).

This isn't just a Google-specific tactic, either. Your clients will love you for it as well. It's always been a general marketing strategy to be likeable: it's the age-old marketing concept that people are more likely to work with those similar to themselves. They see your blog post and say "Hey! This person knows what they're talking about and likes what I like." They see a real person, with a real family, and it makes them feel more comfortable working with you.

A blog is the best place to do this, so plan out your blog structure accordingly. You don't have to do fifty-two weeks of straight specialty on your business or your niche, per se. Every now and then you can do a completely informal, "Hey, somebody asked me about this the other day and I thought I'd talk about it" post.

A good rule of thumb, if you're doing the minimum four times a month, is to split them up half and half. Twice a month goes to business posts, and twice a month goes to local, personal stories. The more people feel they know you personally; the more it will help your conversions and your sales.

This tactic may seem a little too touchy-feely for some, but don't knock it. It works well. Blogging is a great way to drive in clients and improve your ranking, which is of course a major goal of this book for you and your business.

Do not underestimate the power of the local connection.

I've had clients who have followed this process to the letter. Their specialty posts gained a few hits and comments, but it was their local stories and blog posts that became the focal point for them online. Even their "conversations" about how bad traffic during a big event got tons of links, comments and opinions from across the board.

It's a catch twenty-two. You don't get a lot of action on the blog, but it gets your website ranked high on the SERP (Search Engine Result Page), and that's what we wanted in the first place, a high ranking.

Once you rank high on the SERP (Search Engine Result Page), you will get clickers to follow your call to action.

Ultimately, this is what you want. It's the reason for this section of the book and the reason I'm advising you to branch out into your community. Not only does this sort of activity, tied into your locality keywords, mean big index boosts from Google, it also means effective overall marketing. It makes you a real person who other real people feel comfortable calling.

That's about the best advantage over your competition you can have in our modern, skeptical era.

JUST THE FACTS:

- ✓ Blogging is key to the success of your marketing campaign. Make sure to blog at least once a week with a post that is between 250 and 800 words. If possible, blog twice a week. This is the optimal number, but blogging more than twice a week won't help you any more.
- ✓ You don't have to make every blog about your niche or business type. You should alternate between your business and the events in the community.
- ✓ Be natural. This will help you become more accessible to your clients and thus garner more page views and attention from people looking to comment on the blog. It will also make you more viewable and indexable (ranked) by the search engines.

Chapter 5

Let's Get Social: Using Facebook, LinkedIn and the Rest

I know. Some of you are snickering. Some of you are sitting in your home or offices, having read the title of this particular chapter, and are thinking "Twitter. That can't possibly help me."

Don't laugh just yet, however. I know how silly Twitter sounds. I know the derision it's received from all sides, including from our friends and even from the media. The fact of the matter is, however, that Twitter is relevant. As much as it pains me to say it, Twitter may be one of the more important factors to figure in to your Internet marketing strategy.

So you better get tweeting!

Why social media?

Simply put, social media is starting to become a powerful force for Google to determine what is relevant online. The Internet is full of bots (electronic robots), scammers, and article spinners, and many links out there are links to irrelevant or otherwise spammy articles. Social media, however, does the vetting by itself. Users of social media sites aren't going to share the spammy links with each other. They're going to share real content.

As a result, Google has realized that indexing and calculating relevancy from social media is beneficial since social media, in general, has real people posting real content, content that was valuable enough to warrant a "Hey, check this out!" from one person to another.

Some of us have been trying to avoid social media for one reason or another: privacy, general lack of interest, whatever other reason you may have used to avoid it so far. The overall statistics on social media and Internet marketing, however, can't be denied. For example, by 2010 Gen Y has outnumbered Baby Boomers and 96% of them have already joined a social network. These are the people who are looking at the Internet and by ignoring this social media segment; you're basically ignoring their primary mode of access to you.

- The average time on Google is three minutes. The average time on Facebook is thirteen minutes.
- Facebook, as of this writing, has over 1.11 billion users. To put that into perspective, that means Facebook has more people on it than all the people who live in the United States. This is critical in terms of your market saturation.

What these statistics show you is that social media is a powerful force in today's cultural mindset, and it's only getting stronger. Social media is here to stay, and more and more people every day are joining it and receiving advice from their friends and family about great stories or services that they have received from it.

Google has been taking notice of that and responding accordingly, and so should you.

In this chapter, we're going to take a look at social networks and your strategy for them. We're going to figure just how to approach these social media websites and use them to help Google notice you.

The social networks

In the social media game, there are currently three huge players that we're going to focus on: Facebook, Twitter, and LinkedIn. This isn't to say you should ignore the other social media networks out there. They're still important, and in fact location-based social media like Foursquare and Facebook Places are useful too. You may want to have a presence in those, and in other minor social networks, as well, like YouTube, Google+, etc.

For the core of our marketing strategy, however, we're going to focus on the big three. This focus will give you the most coverage and the best ROI in terms of time spent on marketing. So that's how we'll proceed.

Facebook

Facebook is the biggest social media in the room, the 800-pound gorilla. Everybody knows and uses it, so you're going to need to capitalize on that. The first thing you should have is a fan page, and so we'll take a look at how to create one and how to link it into your overall Internet marketing strategy.

TIP:

Many of you may be scared of Facebook's privacy implications. It's important to note that your business fan page is not your personal page. It's not connected to your personal page, it's not the same thing as your personal page, and nothing you post on your personal page will appear on your business page or vice versa. They are completely separate entities.

For any of you who are resisting joining Facebook because you are afraid your fan page will expose your personal page, fear not. None of your personal information will go on your fan page. Your privacy is safe.

Your Facebook Fan Page

A fan page, quite simply, represents your business. Facebook fan pages can have dynamic pages that offer info about your business. You're probably going to want to have someone build a custom i-frame on the landing page for your fan page. Your web developer or webmaster should be able to do this easily. Or you yourself can just go to www.fiverr.com to have someone do it for $5.00.

When new visitors come to your fan page, they will see the information in the i-frame, which will be an opt-in box with benefit information. This is similar to the call to action you have on your main website. "Three things to know before you call an _____," that sort of thing.

The great part of having this fan page is that you're adding new clients onto an email marketing list through a social media channel. It's an organic way of getting warm leads and doing targeted marketing. These people are already in the social media world, surfing around, and in their social network travels; they stumble on your fan page and think "Wow! I might need a service or product you have."

The number one growing demographic on Facebook is the 25-34 and the 35-54 year old female. This is a massive, growing target market of people who need a service or product you have – for all kinds of reasons. It's definitely the right mix of people with the money and the motive to hire a "______," and your fan page on Facebook will be a great place for them to get in touch with you to solve their problem.

While you're creating your Facebook fan page, don't forget about your Facebook Places page, as well. The location-based aspect of this is attractive because of today's proliferation of mobile phones. More and more people are buying smartphones and more and more things are going mobile. With a Places page, people can check in and see what's around them, and you can offer specials through this mode of delivery.

You at least should get on this radar, but you can take it even further. Be creative. Combine things like your Fan page and Places page and figure out ways to synergize the two to make a stronger marketing vehicle overall. The most important thing to know about social media, in general, is that all of these functions can be linked together in different ways. More links equal better ranking.

There are so many options for managing Fan pages and Places pages that it's vital you have a professional who knows how to set up your social media correctly. Barring that, you need to get online and do some extensive research into establishing the proper social media channels. It isn't something you can just cobble together quickly, and you don't want to. You want your social media presence to be as broad and effective as it can be.

Once you've got your Fan page and Places set up, then it's time to move on.

Here is a good example from a lawyer (figure on the next page):

Here is an example of having an opt-in on a Facebook Fan Page

Twitter

Twitter is one of the newest social networks out there and is perhaps the one that triggers the most reluctance to join. It's been vilified by the media and by our peers, but the fact remains that Twitter is the most open social network out there.

That is why Twitter is so important.

Every single tweet (a "tweet" is what each individual Twitter post is called) is indexed by Google. Other social networks, like Facebook and LinkedIn, need a username and password for another to see most of their content. With Twitter, there's no requirement to log in to see individual tweets.

What this means is that Google can index all the tweets out there, and this means that Twitter effects Google page rankings enormously. Google is using people's tweets to help gauge the importance of pages all around the Internet. Pages with lots of links from Twitter, for example, are going to increase their importance. Again, you don't want to be spammy, but you do want to take advantage of this fact.

That's the basis of most of your Twitter interaction, when it's all said and done. You're taking advantage of Twitter's ability to generate constant content without coming across as being spammy. You can't just blast out links to your blog articles all day long, of course. That kind of stream of useless and irrelevant content from you (or rehashed content) isn't going to help you to increase your page rank.

Much like the techniques described in *Go Local Bigtime*, you're going to want to create a bunch of tweets about local events as well enter topical content like minor changes in your business, your inventory, your schedule, changes that would be important or useful for people to know. Your tweets are going to be composed of a similar content to your blogs, except shortened down to the 140 character limit per tweet and sent out once or twice a day.

This may seem as daunting as the blogging, especially considering the daily frequency needed for the tweets. Truth be told, however, 140 characters per entry is not that much at all -- it's about the content of this line and the next -- and you don't have to sit by the computer and send them out one by one. There are tons of websites and programs, like HootSuite (http://hootsuite.com) and SocialOomph (http://www.socialoomph.com), which let you schedule your tweets. You can sit down for an hour and write enough tweets for a week or two, schedule them, and forget about them until the next week when you sit back down to write some more.

Here is a screen shot from the same lawyer above (figure on the next page):

Don't be lazy and be tempted just to tweet an exact duplicate of your blog posts or articles. Your tweets should be about the same content as your blog posts, but they shouldn't be copied and pasted straight from your blog. Google reads those as duplicate content.

What you can do, however, is to link back to your blog from your tweets. In fact, this is not only permissible, it's encouraged. There are many, many plug-ins for countless blogging platforms which enable you to automatically send out a tweet with a link to your blog post every time you post a new blog post. Take advantage of them to generate links to your blog posts. That's not spammy since its only once or twice a week, and it's a great tool for slowly and steadily creating links back to your blog.

There is also plug-ins for Facebook as well. Make sure when you post a blog; its getting automatically posted to your Twitter and Facebook page too.

Here's a tool to "spin" your original content. It takes the original content and rewords the article so the article looks different. Now, when you post on your blog, Twitter, Facebook, etc., the article says the same thing, but the content is written differently in each article. Tricky, huh?

http://www.spinrewriter.com

LinkedIn

In the social media circles, LinkedIn is often completely overshadowed by its bigger social media cousins, Facebook and Twitter. It is often regarded as merely a professional or resume-sharing site and nothing more. This is a big mistake for many. LinkedIn can be an enormous cash cow if used properly.

For starters, LinkedIn itself is no slouch in terms of financial recognition. It is now publicly traded (LNKD), and Linked In has a market cap of $8-$10 billion, which translates to $70 to $100 per user, making it a formidable, fast-growing contender in the social media sphere. Additionally, LinkedIn has an added attraction to us, which isn't related to its market share. Because of LinkedIn's status as a site for professionals and resume-swappers, the average LinkedIn user is far more likely to be a potential client because of the means / motive aspect we described earlier with Facebook.

Some LinkedIn user facts:

1. Over one fifth of users are middle management level or above
2. Almost sixty percent have a college or post grad degree
3. The average household income is $88,573.
4. All of these numbers are higher than the published statistics for the readers of *The Wall Street Journal*, *Forbes*, or *BusinessWeek*.

Put simply, LinkedIn users are wealthier and they have a greater need for your services than the "average" consumer. On LinkedIn, non-useful demographics, like teenagers, aren't crowding user space to post pictures of their friends and pets. LinkedIn is composed of your best potential clients interacting with each other, looking for professionals, and just waiting to be introduced to your business.

Press Releases

This isn't really social media, but I'm going to incorporate it into this section because it deals with controlling a message that goes out and can get shared and can receive comments back. In a sense, the whole medium of the Internet itself is social. Press releases are also one of the few places where Google expects duplicate content, and to Google, the more duplicated and shared the press release is, the more important the content must be.

Here are 15 great press release ideas:

1. **Someone in your company is speaking at an industry conference, local chamber, rotary club, etc.**
2. **You hire someone new into your company**
3. **Someone is promoted**
4. **You join an association (local or national)**
5. **You start offering a new service or product**
6. **New office space or additional office is added**
7. **You have a successful client -- create a Case Study and send out a press release**
8. **Awards have been received or recognition from local or national industry or association has been given**
9. **An employee or officers are named to a charity benefit or a non-profit board**
10. **You have become a large sponsor of a charity benefit**
11. **A new business contract has been awarded to you**

12. **You’re having a big promotion or sweepstakes or contest**

13. **Your product and services tie into a big current event news item (new government law, health discovery, tax time, new hot-topic movie release, etc.)**

14. **You’ve launched a new website (hint, hint)**

15. **There’s been a release of your special report (hint, hint)**

There are both paid and free press sites out there for press releases. The paid press sites are worth the money sometimes because they go out to Associated Press and other big name news wires like Yahoo and Google News. The more your story gets out there, the more possibility it is that it could get picked up locally. A local newspaper could see that press release and pick up the story, for example, and that's a great thing to take advantage of.

The problem of duplicate content as a Google no-no goes out the window here because duplicate content is expected in press releases, and often the big names, like Associated Press and Reuters, even source duplicate content.

As I noted in Chapter Four, this is my favorite distribution site: http://www.spindistribute.com.

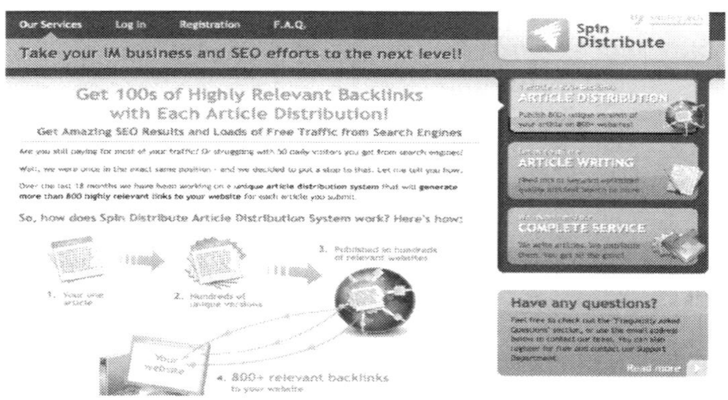

GOOGLE+:

What makes Google+ different from Facebook, Linkedin, Youtube and Twitter?

This is not Google's first attempt at social media. There are many social networks out there, but let's focus on the big four: Facebook, Linkedin, Youtube and Twitter. Understanding how these sites operate helps explain Google+.

Youtube – I make a video. You search for it and can watch, share or comment on it. As a search based network, this is the most open network of them all. Few people use the subscribe function as a social element.

Linkedin – This site started off with "Here is my resume. Please hire me." Now it is "I need a job, I collaborate with my colleagues and vendors to learn and I have grown with the site's groups. I get and answer questions." This the most closed network of the four: you must know my email, already have worked with me, or be in a group with me to connect to me.

Twitter – With this site I can push information out to many people and this information can then be spread further, quickly. A bonus is that Google indexes this network. Any one of the millions of people on Twitter can follow my updates. You can follow me, but I do not need to follow you. Information is sent out in short bursts and any subsequent interaction takes place both on Twitter (in a short conversation style) and off Twitter (after being given a link to see this video, read my blog, etc.).

Facebook - The current king of social media. Facebook is about "friendships." You and I must mutually like each other to share information. I can post information with the hope that this information is seen on your News Feed, but there is actually no guarantee that my information will be seen by my friends. Facebook controls information and uses an algorithm called Edge to determine what information they believe I want to see. There is a great business component with Facebook's Pages (formally fan pages).

What makes Google+ so different?

The big picture is that Google+ is all about connecting every one of your computer activities both online and offline in one place. We are talking cloud on a major scale. We are talking about your documents, spreadsheets, applications, videos, everything, made available in one location. We're talking everything being just one click away from something you can share.

The MAJOR DIFFERENCE of Google+

So this is great then. I can share all my information, everything from my blog to my expense report. However, I don't want to share everything with the world. My mom does not need to know everything about my work and my clients don't want to know everything about my relationship with my mom.

Google+ plus has created a revolutionary function called CIRCLES that controls the stream of information both out and in. People you connect with are organized into different circles.

How does Circles work and why is it important?

1) You can create any kind of circle you want. Examples of my circles might be: Following, Friends, Best Friends, Employees, Clients, Vendors, Very Smart Marketing People, Fellow Auto Repair Marketers, Funny Peeps, Family.

2) The people you connect with can be in multiple circles. Some people that are Very Smart Marketing People can also be in My Friends

3) I can choose to send information to one, or more, circles. This information will appear on their walls or it can be sent as a message. The great thing is that if I share something with my client circle, no one else sees that post on their feed. Maybe I just got back from a family vacation and I want to share the photos with my family and friends, but do not want to bother my vendors, clients, and the general public with the images. I can do that.

4) I can choose to see any information from one or more circles in my feed. Instead of being told what content an algorithm thinks I would like

to see, I can choose my content feed based on my own circles. This allows me to quickly and easily navigate from one set of feeds to the next. Since I can have people in multiple circles, I know that I am seeing what I want from whom I want.

Here are a few other features to Google+

- Multiple Video Chat. Google+ will allow you to connect with up to ten people at the same time on a live video chat. The feature is smooth and the audio is good. It's a great way to connect with people for virtual meetings. The best part of this feature is that only the person who's talking gets highlighted by the main screen.
- There's a larger image and video display on the wall. When you post a video or image, each is about three times larger on the wall compared to a Facebook wall.
- There is easy navigation to all Google functions. While on Google+ you can search the web, see your gmail messages and access your Google Documents.
- There is a "simple share" option, similar to Facebook's. Google uses both a "+1" button (similar to Facebook's "like") and a "share this post" option.
- With just one click you can add someone. If you see a name in a post, find someone in a friend's feed, or stumble upon someone of interest, you can add him or her without navigating to his or her page. This is most convenient. When you hover over their name, a box appears and gives you the option to add them to a circle.

Setting up Google+ is also simple. There are areas for information about you, your pictures, website URL's, and other basic data, similar to the other social media outlets. As with them, too, you only share what you are comfortable sharing. You can include the benefits to working with you and the keywords for your industry (just like on your website) in your "about me" section. Like Linkedin, there is a title area where you can include keywords about your area of practice.

Press releases are so important to your overall online strategy that I've decided this year to start writing, publishing and syndicating releases on behalf of my clients. Once again, I found that the average business owner had better things to do than to write press releases all day. Maybe you have the time, but most of my clients certainly don't. Either way, press releases have to be a part of your overall strategy for success online.

With that, our foray into social media has ended. The next up on our list is directory listings.

JUST THE FACTS:

- ✓ Social media are perhaps the most important force in marketing today. They can't afford to be ignored, and you need to set up strategies for dealing with them.
- ✓ The three biggest social media players right now are Facebook, Twitter and LinkedIn. You need to have pages on each and you need to have a system set up on your blog which pushes blog updates to each of your social networks.
- ✓ Google+, though new, is rapidly growing. Make sure you incorporate it into your marketing strategy.
- ✓ Press releases are a vital part of your online marketing strategy. You should have your marketing firm do them for you to cut down on the immense amount of time you would have to spend on them.
- ✓ Today's social media change rapidly. No single strategy will stay effective forever. Make sure to keep yourself up to date so you can stay ahead of the game.

Chapter 6:

Out with the Old: How to Use Online Directories to Get More Clients

If you've been an Internet user since the pre-search days, you'll know what directory listings are: they're the online versions of the Yellow Pages. These directories -- like Super Pages, YellowPages.com, Yahoo Local, Bing Places, Google Places / Google + Local -- are commonly called "citations" by those in the Internet marketing and search marketing industry. There are hundreds of them across the Internet, but there are only twelve to fifteen major ones where you want to be listed.

In addition to the main directories like MerchantCircle.com, SuperPages.com, Yelp.com, and Yahoo Local, you should be sure to list your business on AVVO.com.

Most of these services allow for a free listing and you should not need anything more than what they provide. Resist the sales calls trying to up-sell you into a paid option of follow-on emails or phone calls. A paid listing or preferred listing could be right for you, depending on your specific market, but do all the free listings first. After you have a baseline for your online success, test the gain in calls or emails you receive by opting for one paid enhancement to a directory listing. That way you can measure the real cost of any benefit from the investment.

Some directories, like InfoUSA, are more influential than others, and you must be sure your information is correct and optimized on them because other directories will pull information from them. In time, as other directories use the information there, your information will proliferate all over the Internet, so make sure it's the right information.

These directories have risen to prominence lately because of Google's local search return policies and because Google has moved its local search returns to its main page by using Google Places / Google + Local. The algorithm that determines which Google Places / Google + Local business listings belong on the first page of Google search results takes a great deal of its weighting consideration by looking around the Internet to see if your business is listed elsewhere. If you're in five, ten or even fifteen directory listings (with reviews in the local area), that's going to look good in Google's ranking system.

We'll get to reviews in the next chapter, but suffice it to say here that directory listings with reviews are essential. If your competition is getting more reviews than you, you often won't make the first page. They will.

You're going to want to be in a great many directories. There are some services out there that will place you in them, but quite often the best way to do it is to do it yourself manually. You want to be in control of this. Some services cut corners in this regard, and they'll slip in shady techniques and insist that you stay out of the process altogether.

It's not that hard to do or that time-consuming, and I recommend doing it manually. Just go through the top ten to fifteen directory listings, enter in your data, place your photos, and fill out the details as fully as you can. A list of the essential directories follows.

Make sure to use keywords and a geolocation in your description. (A geolocation is just an SEO term for your city and state). In keeping with our "tune up" entry, for instance, if you're an auto repair shop and your keywords are "check engine light," you should put "check engine light in Dallas, Texas" into the description of your business.

How to list yourself

It's an easy process to list yourself, all things considered. You just have to go to the directories' websites and follow their relatively simple instructions. Some directories are paid services, but many are free and will only try to "upgrade" and up-charge you with different services once you've listed yourself on the directories. Most of the upgrades and paid directory listings are not necessary.

My experience is that, done correctly, you never need to pay for directory listings or for any of the extra services other than the free ones they offer you. Judicious and skillful use of keywords and geolocations will be more than enough to bump you up to the top. I've had many, many clients top-ranked in Google Places / Google + Local who have never paid for directory listings, and it's most likely the case that you will not ever have to pay for a directory listing or an upgrade either and still do well in the ranking.

That is not to say that these additional paid services might not provide more traffic and clients to your business in the long, but the point is: don't start there.

Be warned, however: you will get multiple phone calls from those directories looking to sell you upgrades and service add-ons. The changes that are now so beneficial to you by Google and other advertising venues online have left many of these directories scrambling by the wayside and rethinking their business models. They may need you to pay for a directory listing, but you may not need to do so right now.

You can safely ignore directories telling you to pay for this upgrade and that upgrade or to pay for their advertising. Stay steadfast, keep on trucking, and you'll see that it wasn't all that necessary to pay for any services that the directory listings "offered" you.

WARNING

This is a *big* warning, and it's a problem I run into with many local businesses.

Sometimes what happens, when you have three or four business partners who are really in one office partnership, is that each of them will go in and create their own listings. You end up inadvertently with multiple listings for each business and one for the office as a whole. When Google queries the directory listings, it gets confused at the multiple entries for the one address, thinks it's an attempt to game the system and ignores them all.

You want to go in and be certain that you only have one listing. To do this, search for your address, business name, other people in the office, anything you can think of, to identify multiple listings. If you find you have multiple listings, and didn't know it, delete them all.

Just get down to zero and start from scratch. It's much better that way. If, for whatever reason you can't delete them all, at least get down to one and edit that one as best you can.

It used to be a clever trick to make duplicate listings to boost search rankings, but now Google cracks down on the practice hard. Remember: duplicate listings are bad. Too many dupes, and Google completely ignores them all. Be wary of this, and search hard to eliminate duplicate listings.

Another important thing to remember when you're doing directory listings is to ensure you use keywords and geolocations only in the short / long descriptions that the directory listings give you. Do not use keywords in your business name. That's why you set up a keyword-rich URL. If the URL had been your business name, you'd have to use that without getting the keyword benefit. Google does not like to see business names stuffed with keywords and geolocations and they'll hurt you in the long run.

It's not impossible to turn this to your advantage, however, depending on how dedicated you are to a closely coordinated, overall marketing strategy. Some of my sharper clients have actually changed their business name to include keywords and geolocations, like "Auto Repair of Georgia Business." It's a bit like the old Yellow Pages game of putting A's in business names to get to the top of the listings, like "AAA Best Dentist of Dallas, Texas."

If your company name officially contains your keywords and location, Google is okay with it. What they are watching for, however, is obvious keyword stuffing like "Jones Smith and Barney auto repair shop – check engine lights - dallas tx." That's bad, and those keywords should only go in your description, not in your business name.

If a directory listing service suggests keywords, consider using them. They'll probably look similar to the Yellow Pages categories you are used to seeing. Some sites give you a chance to type in your own, in which case do so. Don't go crazy, however: Google only values three or four keywords and any beyond that they consider gaming the system and will just ignore them.

Here is a list of directories that your business needs to be listed on.

1. Google Places / Google + Local
2. Yahoo!
3. YellowBot
4. Yelp
5. WhitePages
6. MapQuest
7. SuperPages
8. CitySearch

9. YellowBook

10. Local.com

11. MerchantCircle

There are another forty directory listings that I use with my clients. Some of them are more relevant today than they will be a year from now. Do some research for your own business and business niche and choose about another fifteen directories to list your business on in addition to the core eleven directories above.

Google Places / Google + Local

Google Places / Google + Local, though technically each "a listing," deserve a special mention here.

The Google Places / Google + Local listing should be the absolute last thing you create. Get the rest of your directory listings done first, then wait a month or so until you have a few reviews, and only then create your Google Places / Google + Local page.

The wait time is crucial. In fact, if I meet clients who already have a Google Places / Google + Local listing before the others are in place and the month wait is over, I sometimes advise them to delete the two Google listings and start all over. If they are not already in the top seven listings or not on the first page, I tell them to delete the Google ones, do the other directory listings from the start, and then add Google again a month later.

The reason is that when you create a Google Places / Google + Local page, Google goes out and about on the Internet and looks for all the info already there about you: directory listings, blogs, reviews, and so forth. Doing beforehand all the things I've just talked about should help rocket your way up to the top of the list. In other words, if you want to be on the first page, wait those four weeks before you make a Google Places / Google + Local listing. It makes a huge difference in your ranking.

One other powerful, yet rarely discussed advertising medium is "pay per click" advertising, the best of which is Google AdWords. AdWords is pound-for-pound the single quickest way to get your business listed on the first page of Google.

It'll take you ten minutes or less to do it and it will only cost you a few dollars a day -- when you know what you are doing. Be careful, though. It could cost you thousands a day if you don't know what you're doing.

The key is to have your ads show *only* in your own geographical area. Frankly, my recommendation is to find someone who is skilled at AdWords and pay them to do your ads. It will pay off for you in the end.

JUST THE FACTS:

- ✓ There are hundreds of directory listings out there. Be smart and to start only join the ten or fifteen that are the biggest and the most relevant (yelp, AVVO, etc.).
- ✓ You can pay people to put you on directories, but the best and cheapest way is to do it yourself. Most directories are free. They're going to try to get you with up-sells and add-ons, but don't bother. These don't help.
- ✓ Don't put keywords in your business name in the directories. Google doesn't like that unless those keywords are officially part of your business name.
- ✓ You'll be tempted to put up a Google Places / Google + Local along with the directories, but don't. Since Google pulls information about you when you create the Google Places / Google + Local page, it's best to wait a month or so and create it only after you've gotten a few reviews.

Chapter 7

In with the New: How to Use Online Reviews to Drive Your Marketing

Here's one part of a marketing system, which can confuse some people, especially since reviews are created by their clients and customers. How can reviews make or break a search engine ranking? Sure, they might be helpful for clients talking to clients, but they surely can't influence Google's monstrous ranking machine in your favor.

Can they?

As it turns out, they can, and they do influence the ranking system. Very much, in fact. Google uses reviews, for instance, to judge the validity of the location in question. Put simply, if a location has been reviewed, Google knows someone's been there. Those review comments also give Google an indication of the quality of the location and tell Google whether or not it deserves to be ranked higher or lower.

Many of these reviews allow reviewers to give star ratings, and these are even more influential. Google actually scrapes through these numbers automatically to do a sort of website litmus test to tell whether or not an establishment is an overall positive or negative.

In fact, Google has recently adjusted the Google Places / Google + Local page user interface to prominently display the "Write a review" button in order to encourage specific reviews within Google's own system.

The review sites are, in general, the directory listings we talked about earlier. Google uses their information to determine whether or not you're the best solution to the problem that the search user is trying to solve. That's why it's so important to make Google see that you are, in fact, the best solution to the user's problem. The whole idea of the ranking system, and therefore your marketing strategy, is based on this.

Another key point to this part of your marketing strategy is that many of your competitors are simply not getting reviews at all. This is especially true with most businesses' Internet marketing strategies.

I've recently done extensive research into auto repair shops and hardly any of them are getting any reviews at all. Look at the evidence from this Google Places / Google + Local page:

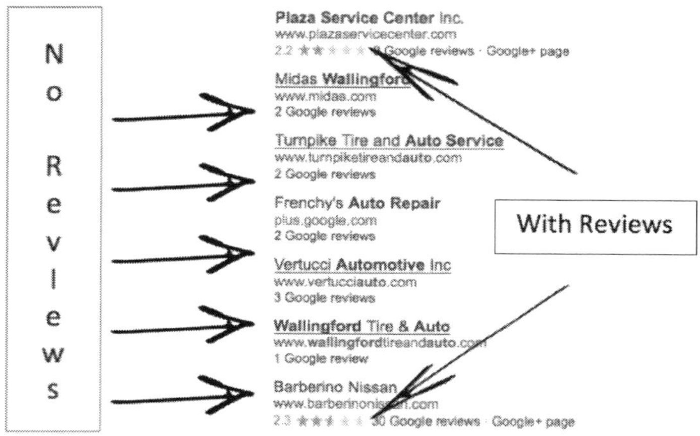

Most of these businesses have no reviews. As you can see only two do.

You can see then that you don't need to get a billion reviews on your directory listings and Google Places / Google + Local page. You just need to have a little consistency and make sure you're getting a couple reviews a month on just two or three of your different directories (one of which must be Google Places / Google + Local).

To start with, you need to size up how many reviews you need to rank. Do some review research with your keywords. Type them into Google and see how many reviews the top ranked results have. If they have five reviews, you need ten. If they have two hundred, well... you've got a lot of work to do.

Typically, however, most small businesses have somewhere in the range of ten to twenty reviews. In some markets I have found, surprisingly, that many businesses don't have any. For the most part, in order to beat your competition in the rankings game, you'll need to have about double the amount of reviews that they have.

Keep in mind that these are the total reviews over time. For example, if you need twenty reviews, you can spread them over four months. That's just five reviews per month, which is certainly doable, and we'll talk about how to get those reviews done in a second.

Review sites

First things first, however.

On which sites should you be focusing on getting reviews? There are tons of them out there, and some of them don't matter and some of them do. How do you figure out which ones are worth your time and which ones aren't?

Thankfully, there's a fairly efficient way to do it. In fact, half the work is already done for you. Many of these review sites are also directory listings, and you've already listed yourself on the top directory listings.

What you have to do, then, is to do a Google keyword search in your location and go through the pages at the bottom. When you scroll down, you'll see numbers as far as the mouse can click. Don't go digging too far, though. You're just interested in the top five directories that are already listed.

Make a list of your directory listings and cross-reference those that appear first in the Google keyword search. For example, if you are an auto repair shop in Denver, Colorado, then you should Google "auto repair – your business name". Then look at the results and find the first three to five listings that refer to an online directory site like Yelp, CitySearch, or SuperPages. The three to five that appear first are the ones you want to focus on.

It's also okay if you don't find five. You may only find two or three at the beginning. That's fine. That's normal. Sometimes it can take search engines quite some time to properly index all the information that's out there.

To give you some perspective, there are about ten thousand new websites created every day. This is a gigantic number for search engines to index, and so often there's a lag time as the search engines crawl the pages and index them. Your mission here is to find the ones that are ranked, and of those, find the top ranked ones.

These are the ones you're going to focus your review techniques on.

Just taking a random name from the above list, “Frenchy’s,” look what comes up:

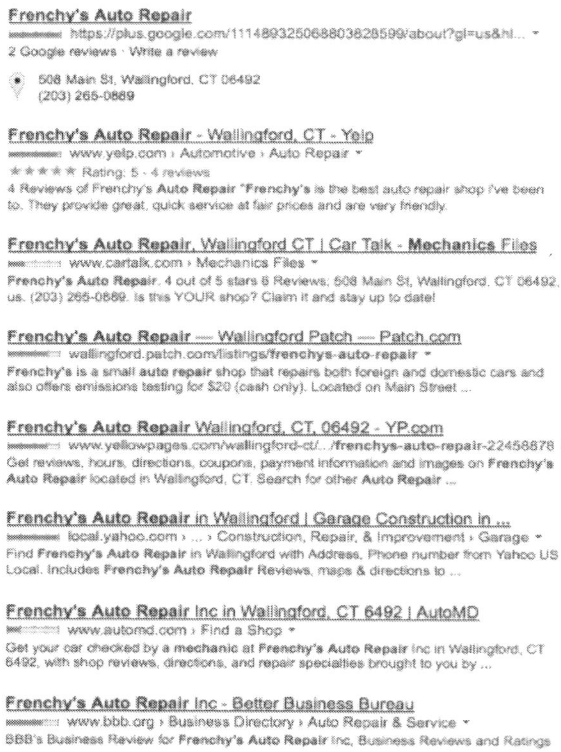

You can see “yelp,” “mechanic files,” patch.com,” YP.com,” AutoMD,” and “Better Business Bureau” all coming up as directories for this auto repair shop.

TIP:

If there are a great number of reviews for your keyword niche, consider focusing on only one or two of them. Ordinarily, a small business like auto repair shops don't have to deal with this since this market isn't saturated with reviews. If you have a competitor who is saturated with reviews, however, Google their keywords and see which review sites are consistently being pulled up the most often. Focus all your review efforts on these.

As an example, if your keyword is "check engine lights" and the majority of reviews are being pulled from CitySearch, then CitySearch is the best place to start.

Getting reviews

Now that we've narrowed down our target directories, let's get reviews on them. We'll start with your current clients. It'll be easier to get reviews from them, as they're right in the middle of working with you.

It's important to note here that we understand that small businesses, depending on the state they're in, are sometimes not allowed to ask for testimonials. You need to understand this: you are not asking for a testimonial. This is important. Be clear to your clients about this point: you are simply asking someone to go to a website and put in a review. A "review" is not a "testimonial. It is an opinion about a business and it could be positive or negative. The review appears on a public forum where they leave the review with or without your assistance.

Now, you can't put a computer in your business and ask for the reviews to be done while someone's visiting your business. The search engines are looking for different IP addresses (Internet Protocol – it is the digital address of your computer) from which these reviews are entered.

You're going to want to have a card produced (see my sample below) that you hand to your clients as they walk out the door. It will tell them where to go and how to write a review.

This is crucial. If you do this, it will make a *huge* difference in your ranking.

Thank you for being a trusted client of ours. Please take a few moments to log into one of these sites and write a quick a review, this will be of great service to us.

- www.Yelp.com/EstatePlanningBoiseID.com
- www.Google.places.com/EstatePlanning BoiseID.com

If you have any questions please contact us directly 555.555.5555

Note - Here is a definition of the ranking system:
★ We completely let you down
★★ There were problems w/ our service
★★★ We could have done better
★★★★ Our services met your expectations
★★★★★ You enjoyed working w/ us

Sample Review For Your Reference:

- "The service was polite and they really made a difficult circumstance comfortable. I am so glad we went to Boise Estate Planning attorney Jane Smith…"
- "I have been working with Boise Estate Planning attorney Jane Smith for years and I am glad to have you in my corner and on my side, thanks for always getting done what you promise"
- "At first I was unsure if I needed any firm. After a few visits I am so glad I chose Boise Estate Planning attorney Jane Smith. Not only did I need a firm Jane really made the whole process painless."

WARNING

You cannot, under any circumstances, go into these websites and create the reviews for your clients. Your clients also can't give you the reviews and have you write them. Google will know from the IP address that these reviews are all coming from the same location and they will ignore them, at best, or get rid of your listing altogether, at worst.

This is true even if these are real reviews that clients have mailed you. A common scammer trick is to have teams of people writing multiple reviews. Google is on to this and is searching that spam out and penalizing the offenders harshly.

Again, under no circumstances should your clients write reviews from your location. They have to go to their computer in their house, their business, or an anonymous coffee shop and write the review there. This is vital. The penalties otherwise are too severe to risk.

This even extends to other computers in your office. Here's a common setup I have seen fairly often. A business will have a "review" computer set up in one office where clients can go and enter in a review. This falls into the same trap as the scenario above, and I always warn clients against this when I see it. Google is tracking these reviews, and even though it's not you typing, unfortunately, it's coming from the same place.

Even though this kind of review is legitimate, Google can't distinguish it from a scammer who employs the same trick. Having a "review station" isn't going to help you at all. Your clients absolutely have to do their reviews on their computers in their home or business.

There's no way around it

2nd WARNING

Be especially careful about who you hire to do your review process. There are many services out there that will solicit you and claim to be able to get you lots of reviews. Too often, these services are near-spam type businesses that just create all the reviews themselves and post them from one IP address. Not only will this not help you, this sort of review fabrication is against the law.

Be careful who you consult and what they say to you. If you talk to a company that says they'll get you twenty reviews in a week, be cautious.

I've seen the reviews from businesses I've worked with that have used such services and their results show twenty reviews for different businesses, but they're all just the same sentence with the business name replaced in each.

Do not use such a service. If you feel you must, make sure you build your process with a proven agency or partner.

I provide my clients with a whitepaper on the entire review process. I also have a process where I do calling and mailers for clients depending on their individual needs. I keep in close communication with the client and continue an active role with them due to the nature, sensitivity and importance of reviews. This is how your service, if you use one, should treat you.

Make sure, too, that your service keeps close to your business while still giving you ultimate control over the review process. This is a crucial part of hiring a service, too.

Because you purchased this book, if you are interested in having one of my partners personally review your website and online strategy, go to http://marketingsuccessfistappointment.com. This URL gives you a coupon that makes the $200 review free for you, since you are reading and implementing the things in this book. Note, while the review is free, I am busy, and its availability may be limited. It's a great opportunity, though, to get your online presence reviewed by an expert.

The best way to get these reviews, as mentioned above, is to hand out your card. Don't stop there, though. Mail or email your clients asking for their reviews (see the sample for lawyers below). It often helps to make it a "team effort" between you and your clients: show them where you're ranking and where your competitors are ranking, and explain that you want to get to the top by getting reviews, as well.

==

Subject:
What does ice cream and Law have in common?

Body:
There are always a million flavors to choose from, but when you find one you like you stick with it. We all have our favorite ice cream and we hope that our firm is your favorite.

We are writing you today to say hello and wish you the best. As part of our efforts to continue to provide the best service to our clients we need to ask you for a quick favor.

Take a moment and go to one of the websites below and leave us a review. This will help us improve and grow as a firm. As a loyal client we want to say thank you in advance.

To make things simple below are a few samples and here is a quick guide to the review process:
Here is a definition of the ranking system:
* We completely let you down
* * There were problems w/ our service
* * * We could have done better
* * * * Our services met your expectations
* * * * * You enjoyed working w/ us

Visit one of these two sites:
http://www.ReviewSiteNumber1.com/yourfirm
http://www.ReviewSiteNumber2.com/yourfirm

Again, thank you.
Best Wishes,
Law Firm of LeBret Homer & Rush
http://www.EstatePlanningAttorneyNoWhereUSA.com

Sample Review For Your Reference:

- "The service was polite and they really made a difficult circumstance comfortable. I am so glad we went to Boise Estate Planning attorney Jane Smith..."
- "I have been working with Boise Estate Planning attorney Jane Smith for years and I am glad to have you in my corner and on my side, thanks for always getting done what you promise"
- "At first I was unsure if I needed any firm. After a few visits I am so glad I chose Boise Estate Planning attorney Jane Smith. Not only did I need a firm Jane really made the whole process painless."

==

Remember that this isn't all about Google Places / Google + Local. Send reviews to a few different directories. You do, of course, want reviews going to Google Places / Google + Local, but you need to diversify. Send out cards with other review sites on them as well, such as Yelp, CitySearch and others that you've identified in your target directory listings.

Don't put them all onto one card, however. That will look cramped, awkward and unprofessional. One card per review site looks much better, and it'll work better in getting clients to go to the review sites for you.

The same goes for your email. Your clients may already have an account on one of these review sites and in that case it would be even easier for them to leave a review saying what a wonderful job you did. This will help you even more because identified reviews count even more than anonymous ones.

Again, it's important to note that these reviews are absolutely, positively not testimonials. These are things that consumers can go and do on their own. You're simply trying to encourage a behavior that is already happening on the Internet. Don't be surprised if, when you start this process, you find you already have a couple of reviews scattered around the Internet.

Say to your clients, "Hey, there are these review sites out there and having reviews help us. You might do it already, and if you liked our service, your review will really help our Internet ranking and get more people into our door."

You'll find, more often than not, that people are more than willing to help you out. They'll go to these sites and fill out reviews, and this is one of the driving forces behind the Google Places / Google + Local rankings.

By having a steady system of reviews, you're ensuring your steady climb to the top.

This is where you get to independently tell our other clients and prospects whether we met your expectations

JUST THE FACTS:

- ✓ Reviews are important and should not be overlooked. Search the review sites and find out which ones you should be focusing on.
- ✓ Make sure you have a system in place to get users to review you. Remember, these are not testimonials.
- ✓ Whatever you do, don't have a computer in your office for clients to write reviews on (and absolutely don't write their reviews for them). Google requires the reviews to be written by the client on a computer outside of the office, so the reviews need to be done on the client's own computer.
- ✓ Be careful about who you hire to do your review marketing. Some marketers will promise huge numbers, but write fake reviews with duplicate content and end up severely damage your Google ranking.

Chapter 8

Automation: How to Get Robots to Do Your Work for You

Follow-up strategies are a vital segment of any Internet marketing strategy, and it's equally vital that you automate them as much as possible. Many businesses try to do them manually, but the overhead required to manually implement following up isn't feasible for most businesses.

You can't spend all that time manually fielding emails and responding to them one by one.

I've had clients in the past who literally sent out hundreds of e-mail newsletters every week by hand. If somebody new came in, they'd get manually added to this email list. That sort of system may work in the beginning, but it's easy to see that it doesn't scale up well at all. You'll need an automated method of follow-up, which both preserves quality and scales out well, freeing up resources and keeping your Internet marketing strategy running smoothly and efficiently.

Follow-up framework

We have to talk first about the framework for follow-up. When we're talking about follow-up, we're talking about traffic generated to you. We're not talking about people that come in through the door. We're talking about follow-up that happens when the person finds you and you need a follow-up strategy whether or not the contact is initiated by phone, email or online via the website or blog.

When a new client gets to your website and chooses to give you their name, phone number and email address, they go into your "funnel." A funnel is the resource you have where you capture your leads and market to them specifically from there. The reason for this is that they've gone through the trouble of giving you this information -- they're a "warm lead" and obviously interested -- and you have to get back to them fast. The whole function of the funnel is to provide you with a resource that enables this sort of rapid response to whatever communication a client or potential client initiates.

The best way to do this is to set up a basic autoresponder system. This system will provide two things for you: it's going to alert you that someone's given you information, and it's going to send them back a message immediately.

There are a couple of ways to do this -- and later on we'll talk about other techniques, including texting and direct voicemail – but the most traditional and common autoresponse is an email. They should get one immediately.

A typical autoresponse email could look something like this:

Hi Mark,

Somehow not all vanilla ice-cream is created equal. In fact, in my opinion, there are plenty of cartons that shouldn't even be allowed to call themselves vanilla.

Finding the right attorney to help you can be like picking out vanilla ice-cream for the 1st time...

You are not 100% sure you are getting what you need for the situation you have.

Sometimes what you really need is more information before you make any decision.

There is a reason you still have not made any decisions and my report may not have answered all your questions. I find that every situation is a little different and I would almost 100% guarantee that your personal situation is unique and needs answers beyond what you already have.

Of course there are not enough hours in a week for me to talk to everyone with a question, and I wish I could, so I can't say that I will be able to connect with you today, but give my office a call and ask for when the next opening is on our firm's calendar.

We can spend 15 minutes on the phone and a lawyer from our firm will personally answer questions you have about elder law and working with attorneys.

Just tell the person that answers that I sent you this email and said it was ok that we scheduled a call this week or next.

We are here to help you with this process. Until we talk to you, have a great day.

All The Best,

They should get a response immediately after they've submitted their information to your web page.

There are many services out there that provide these types of autoresponding systems: Constant Contact, AWeber, InfusionSoft, iContact, and Mail Chimp for example. Whichever service you go with, you have to make absolutely sure that they have a system in place capable of capturing names, storing names in an organized way, and making it as easy and automated as possible to send out those autoresponders.

You need to have a separate strategy in place for phone numbers. If someone gives you their phone number, you should not only email them right away, but also email someone in your office right away with a note that says, "Hey, this person called and they're interested in this. Here's their number."

The reason for this is that the Internet is a 24/7 operation. It doesn't close, it's always open, and your website is happily receiving visitors all around the clock. Your office hours, however, are only during the day. If your office hours are nine to four, for example, you won't be answering phones at ten in the evening. Hosted Number (mentioned earlier) can help you with this. It has "find me," and "office hours" features to make this easier. (www.hostednumbers.com)

The reason for emailing your office member is that if someone contacts you at night and submits their information, they get an immediate email. When your person gets in the next morning at nine, they can see the email and know someone tried to get in touch. They can then pick up the phone and say "Hey, this is Bob Jones from Jones, Smith, and Johnson. I see you downloaded our special report. I hope it helped you out. I'm just calling to ask if there's anything we can help you with."

This is a personal follow-up to a warm lead -- with an emphasis on the personal. I can't stress that enough -- you're a local business providing a service to the community and you need to reach out and make those personal connections. The bigger the personal step you take, the better. An automated email is the minimum bar to entry. If they've gone through the trouble of giving you their email, you need to say thanks, email back, and throw in a special report. Then maybe email them again a few days later with another message.

All this needs to be automated. You can have a few different templates for any email you send out to these warm leads.

It's important to implement this email / phone call system and use it regularly. This isn't
e-commerce, of course. We're not going to close any deals online. There's no shopping cart, no impulse buy button that's going to magically give you clients without any legwork. You are still a local business, engaged in local Internet marketing.

You can't just send out an email and expect things to happen. You'll need to get that phone call or office visit to seal the deal.

Another good practice is to email out one of your blog posts each month. Just take one of your blog posts, any one of them, and fire it out each month to anyone on your email lists. It's also easy to send out what's called a "broadcast message" to anyone who's on your email list and is still marked as open to receiving communication from you.

You want to do this because, on the whole, any Internet marketing strategy is a long-term strategy. Your clients may be thinking they need legal services or a tune up, but they may not need them right at this moment. They will need them down the line, though, and these periodic emails will let them remember who you are.

This is called "top of mind awareness" in marketing. You want to be on the top of your client's mind down the road. They may one day think "Oh! My dad needs info about his check engine light. I've been getting these emails from a business that's right down the road and they deal with this sort of thing. Maybe I'll give them a call and see if they can answer my questions."

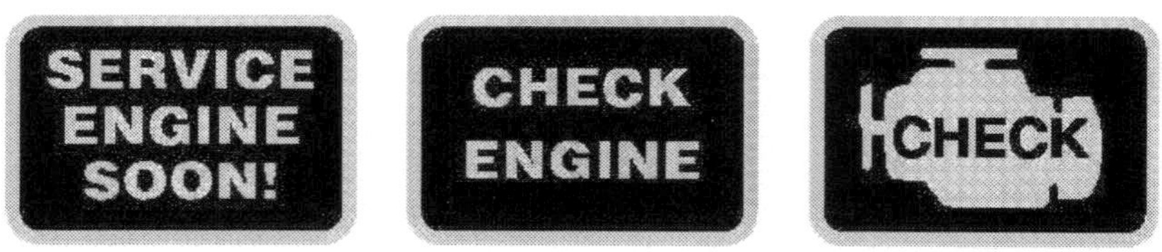

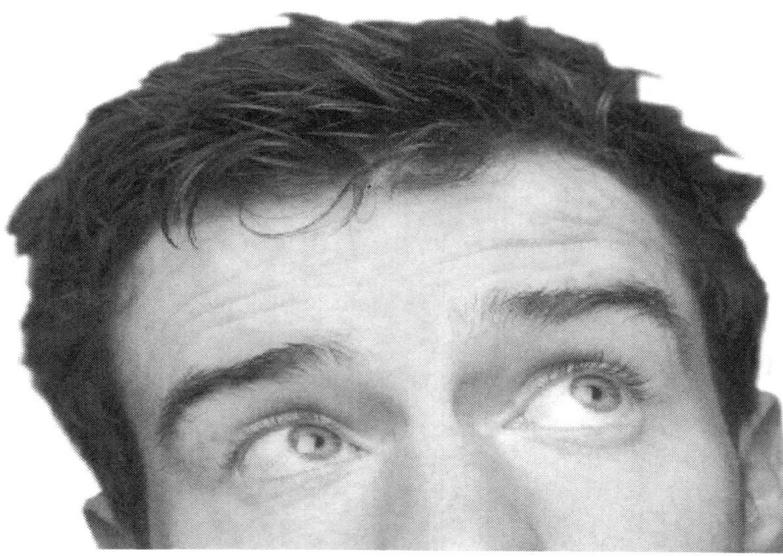

JUST THE FACTS:

- ✓ Follow-up is important, but it's equally important that your follow-up process be automated. No one should be sending out newsletters or follow-ups by hand, nor manually adding anyone to lists.
- ✓ Don't just follow-up with your leads when they fill out a form. Follow-up in the office as well. This lets an employee call leads as soon as possible, while they're still warm, and show them that you're friendly and ready to do business.
- ✓ It's important to keep regular contact with your clients. Fire off a blog post once a month to your email lists in order to keep your business in the forefront of their minds.

Chapter 9

The Bottom Line: ROI and How to Be Sure You Make More Than You Spend

In too many of the "typical" advertising solutions I've seen with my clients, most of their ad dollars get spent in the Yellow Pages, along with some TV and some radio or newspaper print. They're usually not spending much money online, and if they are, it's an extension of the Yellow Pages that's usually not well-tracked and too often is ineffective.

Advertising online, however, has a huge advantage over traditional advertising methods used by most businesses. It's extraordinarily easy to track what's going on throughout the entire online process.

You can track pretty well what's happening in each stage of the game: who emailed, what's in the funnel, who's been autoresponded to, what's their response been, etc. This is difficult to do with regular advertising. Quite often the only means of communication to a new prospect which traditional advertising media gives you is a phone number. Unless you're asking them where they heard about you or you're creating a unique phone number for each ad -- which is, by the way, the best practice, and more on that later -- you're not getting good information at all about how your advertising budget is helping you.

Unless, of course, you have already taken my advice about using www.hostednumbers.com to track your off line marketing activities. This definitely beats asking every customer how he or she heard of you. Most won't remember. And it is hard, and expensive, to get staff to do it. That's the "old" way of tracking.

In contrast to traditional advertising methods, you can glean vast amounts of data from the Internet and the tools available to you for it. You can track how many people visit and what keywords they typed in that led them to clicking your site. If they visit your Google Places / Google + Local page, you can have instant data about who visited, when, and how. Some directory listings have their own tracking data in place, as well.

The Big Kahuna in this realm, however, is Google Analytics.

Google Analytics is an absolute must-have for your website. If it's not already on your website, ask your webmaster to integrate Google Analytics with your site. If he can't, it's time to find another webmaster. That's how important Google Analytics is to your ROI (Return on Investment). It tells you who's visiting, who's clicking, what data they're entering, how well your website is converting leads, how long your clients stay on your site, and more.

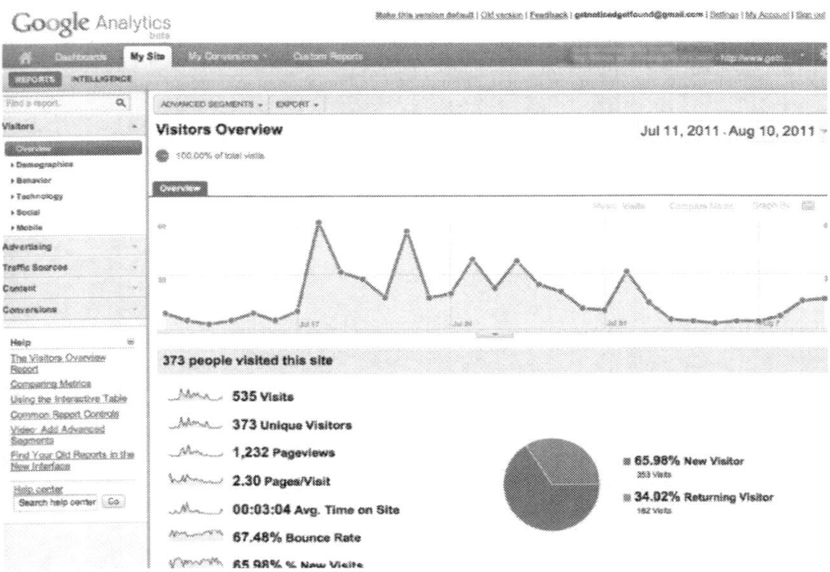

It's the essential tool for monitoring your ROI and your website, and it needs to be there.

Say you're an auto repair shop, not an online marketing geek. While tracking hits and calls is important -- you do need to know where your money is going -- I find that most small businesses just don't have the time to track their marketing on a consistent basis. That's why I implemented a system for my private clients where I track all traffic on their website…and all of the calls to their office. At the end of each month, they get a detailed report on all of the action.

I mentioned above having different phone numbers for each print, radio or TV ad. That's cumbersome, and you can accomplish that kind of tracking far more easily online. For example, there are services online that allow you to create different unique forwarding numbers that all forward to your actual number. The only difference is that the call statistics are online and you can easily see at a glance how many calls each number receives. That doesn't mean you have to get rid of your current phone number. In fact, you shouldn't. These numbers are only forwarding numbers and nothing more. Clients with your old number can still get through perfectly well on your regular number.

Another great tool is Google Webmaster Tools. It tells you how many people are linking to you across the Internet and thus how well your Internet marketing strategy is doing overall. This should be complemented with statistics on your email funnel and your autoresponders. You should be able to see how many people are getting and opening your emails so you can keep track of that as well.

On top of all that, you'll get your own internal CRM (Customer Relationship Management system). It calculates how much money you're charging, how long you're working, how long you spend with each client, and so forth. As we'll see, that's an incredibly key resource for determining your ROI.

On that note, we're assuming that you already have some sort of internal CRM in place. It is crucial. Discussing the complete process and all the tools needed to manage internal CRM is beyond the scope of this book, but there are many resources available to provide you help and support with implementing your own CRM. Suffice it to say, it's a vital step in the chain, and you need to have one before you can accurately calculate your ROI.

Today there are an almost unlimited number of things you can track online in order to measure your ROI. If you're going to take anything away from this section it is this: it's imperative that you have a strong, stable, well-defined system in place in order to correctly track your ROI. Most of the clients I work with believe they have a process in place, but when their "system" is subjected to a rigorous examination, it usually breaks down. It's a good first step, of course, that they even have a system in place.

It's good business sense and standard marketing practice. You're spending money, and you want to know where that money's going and how that money's helping you. But your ROI tracking has to be complete and it has to work. For an Internet marketing strategy, however, you need to go above and beyond the rudimentary. You need to be taking in the data that show you the points of entry for all your clients.

An example of a monthly run-down might look something like this. In total, 155 people visited our site this month. Of those visits, 35 came from Google Places / Google + Local, 120 from Google organic search, and 12 from Facebook fan pages. Of these 155 visits, we followed up with all of them. Of the clients we followed up with, we closed 45, and each one of them was worth, on average, $1200 of our products or services.

This is basic, and these numbers are simply example numbers, but it should give you an idea of how you should be looking at and tracking your Internet marketing. This tool allows you to get an accurate sense of valuation from the clients who have found you online. You need to know: Are they worth the same amount as clients who found you driving by or from referrals?

Capturing ROI information from those clients online is important, and I find I often have to build up new systems and processes for clients so they can get this reporting accurately. Make absolutely sure that when planning out your overall Internet marketing strategy, you decide what metrics you're going to use and just how you're going to track them.

I can't stress this point enough: it's vital that you have an understanding of your ROI online all the time. Efficient and accurate monitoring in this realm gives you an unparalleled advantage over traditional media. You can know down to the dollar whether your spending in the online arena is good for your ROI. In fact, I tell most of my clients that if they're not getting at least three times their ROI on their Internet marketing, something is really wrong.

Usually, the return is far more than that. Three times the ROI is the bare minimum my clients see. If you're not getting that, it means you need to go back and look again at your strategy. Either you've missed something along the way or you're in a particularly competitive market and you need to bring in a second opinion or another expert to help you fully break into your market.

Tracking your own ROI gives you one other large advantage: should you choose to hire a marketing agency for your Internet marketing, you can tell whether or not the marketing agency you hired is working well or not, and you'll know whether you should stick with them or find someone new.

TIP:

If you're working with an agency, you should require them to provide you with these ROI reports. They can get them, and if they're not giving them to you or claim they're unable to get them, there's something wrong. They're either hiding something or they're simply not as good as you thought they were.

Understanding your ROI, understanding your analytics, using online-only phone numbers, all of these things simply underscore the philosophy that you should always adhere to in your online Internet marketing strategy: use every tool and resource available to you so you know where your dollars are going and whether or not your online advertising dollars are pulling their weight. The more control you have over your information flow and over your tracking information, the more valuable your online strategy is going to be and, ultimately, the more valuable your business as a whole will become.

JUST THE FACTS:

- ✓ ROI tracking for print, radio and TV ads is scarce and generally ineffectual. Online ROI tracking is easy, offers a wealth of information and enables you to precisely track where your money is going and how much of it is coming back.
- ✓ It's imperative that you have a strong, stable, well-defined system in place in order to correctly track your ROI. At the very least, know where your money is going, know what sites are giving you hits, know what percentage of leads you're converting, from which sites, and know how much on average you're converting them for. .
- ✓ If you work with a marketing agency, it's vital that they give you these ROI reports. They can give them, and if they can't or don't want to, something is wrong.

Chapter 10

Where Do I Go from Here?

If you've reached this chapter, give yourself a pat on the back: you've done more for your online Internet marketing strategy than most local businesses will ever do.

You've now got a solid foundation for pulling clients in from the web. You're ranked high with a no-nonsense website that calls prospects to action. You're a Facebook and Twitter regular, and you have in place a sophisticated system of follow-ups and ROI tracking that will enable you to pinpoint your highest-profit channels with incredible accuracy.

That's still no reason to get complacent, however. The Internet is, by its nature, a fast-moving target. Internet marketing isn't always going to stay in stasis, and you'll have to work to keep up with it. With that in mind, this chapter is dedicated to what's coming down the road. There are things that have not yet become major players in online marketing, but they absolutely will be down the line. These are things that a local business has to think about, the new technologies and new trends that will have to be incorporated into your marketing strategy in order to keep at the top of your game.

Here are some hints of what to keep in your sights:

Mobile

I've held this particular topic to the end, but this is perhaps the most immediate of all the coming challenges for Internet marketing. Mobile devices are rapidly becoming the primary mode of interaction with the Internet. Mary Meeker of Morgan-Stanley has recently estimated that, given current mobile trends, the number of mobile devices that connect to the Internet will eclipse that of regular desktop PC's and laptops by mid-2013. You heard that right: by 2014, more people will be connecting to the Internet by phone than by computer. In fact, mobile is already a driving force behind many of the search engine changes we've seen. Google, for example, is setting up its local places infrastructure because it believes information is going mobile.

Mobile search is a different creature than traditional search. It's more often an immediate need. Users who search mobile are typically driven by an "I need something right now that's near me" mentality, as opposed to a more research-oriented desktop user who's willing to sift through answers and Wikipedia articles. Few people will be doing that on a mobile phone. Most will be looking for a business nearby which they can walk or drive to quickly.

Many small businesses have looked skeptically at me when I've said this is great news for small business owners, but it is. People are out at lunch, driving around, or talking about stuff and think of their problem. More and more, they'll just think to themselves, "Oh! I'll just use my phone really quick and search for an answer." The same applies when they're sitting around eating dinner or watching TV. Chances are they have their iPhone, Android phone or tablet sitting right next to them. Instead of waiting and looking up the answer to their problem later on a computer, they'll just pick up their mobile device and look for the answer right then and there.

The business that's right near by will benefit. Hopefully, that's you.

This might seem far-fetched, but it's not. Think about your own mobile smartphone use or the usage patterns you've observed in others. People are typing in searches all over the place. There's a clear aura of instant gratification with any sort of mobile device, and users take advantage of it to get an instant answer. If your site's not mobile-friendly or your Google Places / Google + Local page is non-existent -- by the way, Google Places / Google + Local is extremely mobile friendly -- then you're going to get left out in the cold.

The mobile realm also tightens up the ranking requirements quite a bit. On the regular desktop Internet, you've got to be in the top seven rankings. It'd be nice to be in the top three or four, but seven's the bare minimum. On mobile devices, if you're not in the top two, you're not being seen. Few people scroll down on mobile phones, and often they simply tap the first or second result they see. More instant gratification.

This is important to you because mobile phones offer an unparalleled ease of use. For example, many phones like iPhone and Android offer built-in calling from the web. Users can simply tap a finger on their phone number and the smartphone dials the number automatically, without any need to ever pick up another phone. As mobile devices become more and more common, it's of critical importance that your site is mobile-friendly and sits in that number one or number two listing on Google's result returns.

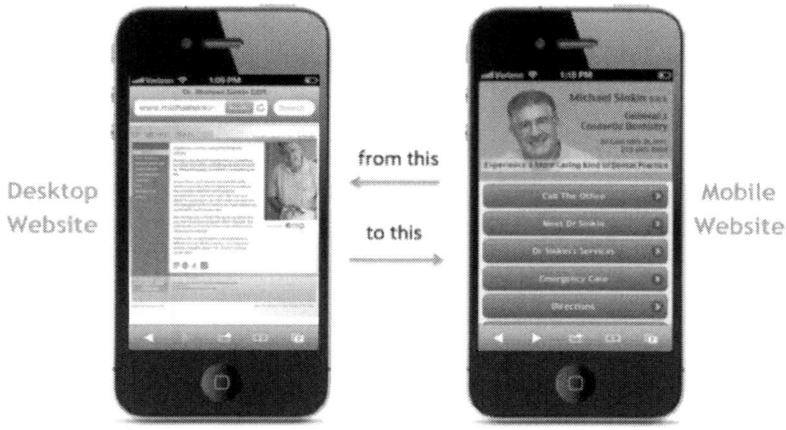

As you can see from this illustration, it is much easier for a prospect to use a website made for the cell phone device. It is well worth the added expense for any website to have this feature.

Social

I've covered a great deal about social media previously, and you're well-equipped to handle the social network scene at the moment. What I didn't cover, however, is the future of social networks: how they're going to change and how that's going to impact your overall online marketing strategy.

The first and most important aspect of future social is that eventually social media services are going to be more than just places where people connect. In the future, social media networks are going to transform into something more search engine oriented. People will go to Facebook not just to interact, but to search for things, as well. This makes it crucial that you have an established presence early on.

It is not too late, and you are not behind the curve. Start having a presence on sites like LinkedIn, Twitter, Facebook, YouTube, StumbleUpon, Digg, and other social media sites. This doesn't mean you have to interact with all of these social media networks every day or even frequently, although you're going to want to keep more in touch with the big ones, as I noted in the social network chapter. What you do want, however, is a presence. Make sure that you have listings on these websites. You'll be glad you did down the road.

Social networks are also getting more location-oriented as time goes on, and I expect that trend to continue. This will eventually lead to a sort of social-mobile combo: users who are Google searching while also in their Facebook mobile app. This has already become a pattern for many users, and I expect a rise in this behavior in the future. Users are in their Facebook app and just go to the places listings to see what's around them.

Your first reaction is probably that this makes the most sense for restaurants and bars, and it's true: they've already started to capitalize on this. However, this is useful for other businesses as well. Users can note "Oh, this is where so-and-so's office is" and they'll remember it. You need to have this local presence, because if you're not there and you're not found, someone else will be.

This social / search hybrid that I'm seeing slowly crop up will form another important piece of Internet marketing going forward: a combination of social word-of-mouth and Google ranking. Instead of letting Google figure out who's first, more and more people are going to go to Facebook to see what their friends think.

Your interaction level, reviews and presence on Facebook are going to be crucial at this stage of the game. People are going to search on Facebook the way they're currently searching on Google. Some Internet results will still trickle through, but for the most part the results will come from the client's social networks.

This is important because people take their friends' and family's opinions about businesses seriously. From a marketing perspective, it's a long-known and often proven fact that people give far more weight to opinions from friends and family than from any other source of marketing. It's the best word-of-mouth. As a result, these combos of social media searching are going to be increasingly influential, and you should keep an eye on them and stay on top of them as they progress.

Direct Mailing to Online Source

You may wonder why I'm putting direct mailing in the "What's Next" category. In Internet marketing terms, direct mailing is older than dust. The reason it's here is that there's more potential for it again as the years roll on. Like fashion from the seventies coming back around and becoming popular again, direct mailing is making a comeback.

The reason for this is partly because of its scarcity. Receiving mail every now and then, done properly, is not a poor marketing option. It's not something you should rely on heavily, but it's definitely something to keep in your arsenal and use where it's appropriate.

If you already have a direct mail campaign going and want to keep doing it, you need to find a way to incorporate into your direct mailers Google Places / Google + Local, Facebook, your website, or a call to action. Today you have to shift your direct mailing goal to getting people online first. Direct mailing with mobile is an especially attractive option: being able to snap a picture and go straight to a website to see info or reviews or being able to text a certain number to get a special report are options that look more promising in the near future.

Texting

As mentioned with direct mailing, you can now have people text a number to receive information. In fact, they're actually entering your marketing funnel the moment they text that number. This is all automatic, too. You can have the same autoresponder system set up so that it sends texts in the same way that it sends emails. If a user puts in their mobile phone number, they get a text that says something like "We've received your name and email. Thank you very much for getting in contact. Check your email for a special report, free of charge. One of our representatives will be in touch."

There is one other aspect about texting that should be mentioned here. Some in the restaurant and bar business have automatic texts that send the latest coupons or deals: Tuesday happy hours, Five for Four Fridays, lunch specials, and other marketing ploys like that. Although it has become common in the restaurant and bar scene, I've only started to implement some of those texting ideas with my small business clients. The truth be told, I'm not sure if it will be taken as spammy or not, but depending on your niche, it might work for you. Text me at (203) 779-7400 to see what I am speaking about, and how it works.

Once someone gives you their mobile phone number, don't be afraid to send out texts once or twice a month. Make sure the texts are useful, and don't send them more than once or twice each month. That could start to feel spammy for them. Texts are read over 90% of the time once they're received, as opposed to emails, which are read only 17-20% of the time (and those are optimistic numbers).

A well-placed, well-timed text or two every now and then can really help drum up new business and get clients to call you.

Direct Voicemail

Direct voicemail is the practice of sending a voicemail directly to a phone without the phone ever ringing. This is technically possible to do now with mobile phone voicemail systems, and in actuality it works well. These systems are nifty: you can set up outbound voicemails that talk about something new or something local that you and your business did. The voicemail can be about thirty to ninety seconds, and instead of calling them, you can send it directly to their phone. It's efficient. The voicemail notifier pops up, but the phone never rings, meaning the client can see the voicemail message and listen whenever they want to. It's non-intrusive and as a result, the listen rate is much higher.

This is one of the reasons I recommended earlier to get mobile phone numbers from your leads. It not only opens up the texting avenue, but this direct voicemail avenue as well.

Direct voicemail is personal and effective, and it's best used for events or other local things your business might be doing. One example might be seminars. If you do seminars in the area about topics relevant to your business, dropping a direct voicemail to each of your clients is a great, personal way to let them know about your upcoming seminars. It's easy, non-intrusive, and it works.

Summing Up

I called this chapter "What's Next" for a reason. Many of these technologies are going to effect or are already beginning to effect the Internet marketing arena. Some of these ideas and strategies are already in play and I've begun to experiment with them for some of my clients who are ahead of the curve or are battling in especially competitive markets.

In other words, these new ideas are not simply theory or fluff. They're real strategies that are beginning to come into the market, and it's a good idea to keep abreast of them going forward.

Talk to the agency that you're working with and see what their ideas are about these future strategies. Nothing's set in stone with them, and a creative idea or two could really put you ahead in these arenas. It's also important that you find the right agency, one that specializes in these techniques. These may not all be things your average webmaster knows how to do, and chances are some webmasters haven't even heard of them.

Make sure you talk to an agency or service that thoroughly understands the full realm of Internet marketing and how it works with other marketing. They need to be aware of future strategies, too, which will be coming down the line.

For more help, be sure to visit my website, too: http://marketingsuccessfistappointment.com

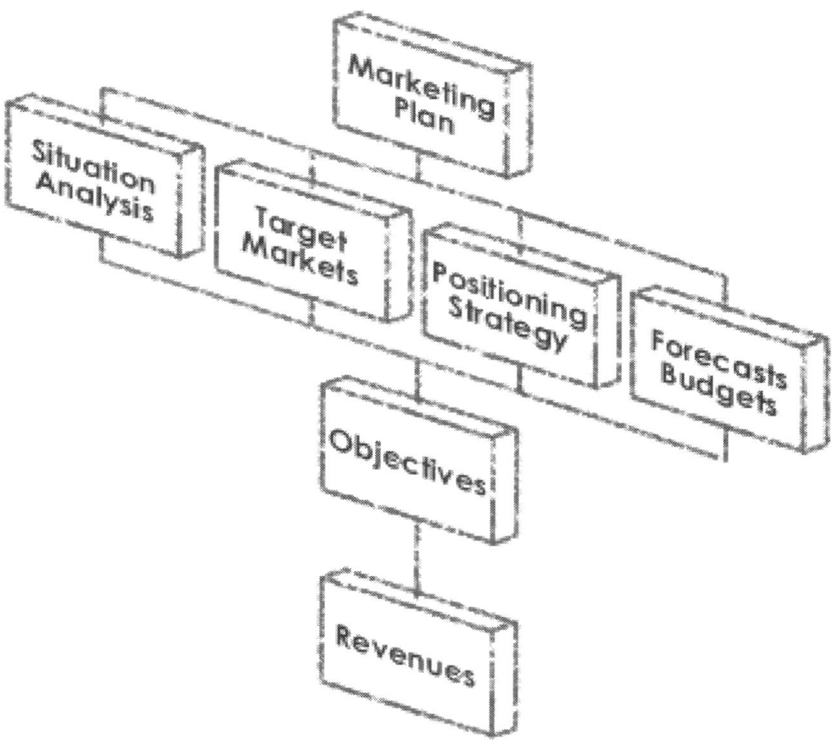

JUST THE FACTS:

- ✓ Mobile and social media are going to be the driving forces in marketing over the next few years. Both are already driving marketing to become more location-oriented because of the "always on" nature that combines and unites mobile and social. Keep up to date on them and don't miss any opportunities to be creative and capitalize on these markets.
- ✓ People give much stronger weight to opinions from friends. Make sure you have a strong social presence, and leverage that social presence by having a well-established business that will rank high in the inevitable search / social hybrid arena.
- ✓ Direct mailing still has a place in the world, but it should be driving clients to your website to get that warm lead and -- more importantly -- get them to use a channel that's more easily tracked and analyzed.
- ✓ Don't ever be complacent. Always think of new ways to innovate with and incorporate these new technologies. Make sure, too, that you're working with agencies that have a good feel for the online field, are specialists in the online marketing world, and know how to help you stay at the top of your game.

Chapter 11

How to Get Help Getting All of This Done

The last thing you're going to need is to train a new workforce for all this.

Let's face it, you didn't go to school, learn your craft, and build your business just so you could spend eleven non-billable hours a day uploading videos, submitting listings to directories and designing websites. Or teaching someone else to.

Now I really wish I had better news for you, but finding competent people to do this work for you will not be easy. Most web designers are broke, they know nothing about marketing, and many don't have any clients outside of your local city. And yes, they often do live in their parent's basement. This is not the kind of person you can trust with your marketing budget so be thorough in researching who to invest with.

I get asked all the time where to find a good web person. My answer is that every time I find one who knows what they are doing (they are rare), I hire them to work on my team.

Outsourcing this work to India or to some fly-by-night business will create more work for you than it will save, and having one of your clerks or assistants do this work will drive you both crazy and possibly ruin your working relationship.

So How Can I Get All of This Done?

First, by now you'll agree that local web marketing is probably the most time-sensitive, urgent issue on your business calendar today. If you look back on this book six, twelve or even eighteen months from now and you've done nothing, you'll wish you had a time machine to transport you back to today so you *can* start now.

The local Internet marketing door is wide open right now, but it is closing fast. You don't want to miss out on securing the financial future of your business just because you had a big workload this week.

On the other hand, it is difficult to find good people to help you with your online presence. Web designers can be flakes. Even if they knew how to put up a good site, it doesn't mean they can get you on page #1 of Google multiple times. Outsourcing this kind of work to India or the Philippines is a waste of time and money. (I've tried it and I won't make that mistake again).

I would love to offer the services of my marketing agency, but at the time of this writing, I am full with my current paying clients…and my commitment is to them.

In the interest of full disclosure, though, I do provide a turnkey, 100% Done-For-You service. You send us your business contact information and we do the rest. It's literally *all* done for you and I know how to get results faster than anyone.

My services are expensive, and you will probably be able to find someone to do a bare-bones job for much less. I do invest a lot of money into my client's future, though, and when you get three, five, or nine or more clients per month each buying $5,000.00 of your products or services, we all win.

I'm currently restricting myself to only a handful of clients in any given geographical area. Your area may already be spoken for and while that's not to say I won't take you, there's a good chance I will already be committed there and have to pass.

Having said all of that, if you feel that you are a business that I should choose to work with and you would like to find out about my team's availability to help you get all of this done *for you*, please contact me at:

Phone: (203) 779-7400

Fax: (203) 774-1015

Web: http://marketingsuccessfistappointment.com
Or text the keyword firstappointment, your name and your email to 58885

I will, at the very least, be able to tell you if I am already working with a business like yours in your area.

If I decide to move forward with you, I always start with my 22 Point Web Strategy Diagnosis. Or my 60-90 marketing analysis. Whichever makes most sense to you? There is no obligation on either your or my part at this point. The diagnosis just begins a discussion about how we may be able to help you.

While I know that some people take these experience-backed, high-quality web strategies from me and then go and hire a cheap local marketing agency, I also know that the best customers -- those who understand the value of growing their business by maximizing their online marketing investment -- will ask me to just "do it for me."

I am looking for a small number of clients to build a long-term relationship with. If that sounds like your business, then please do feel free to write or call.

With that, I bid you adieu. You've reached the end of this book, but you certainly haven't reached the end of how I can help you. If you've followed all the techniques and processes in this book and taken them to heart, you're prepared to wade into the online marketing arena and come out the victor.

You're ahead of most of your competitors and you have a clear idea of what lies in store. Don't get complacent. Implement, be creative, and you'll be successful in the online marketing arena for many years to come.

APPENDIX A: GLOSSARY

ANALYTICS: Analytics are technical measures you can take to see what happens with visitors on your website: how long they stay, what they click, how many of them return to the website, and statistics of that nature. One of the best analytic software packages out there currently is Google Analytics, which is free.

AUTORESPONDER: An autoresponder is a system put in place to automatically respond to communication initiated by a potential client, usually via email. Autoresponders can range from simple to extremely complex and can either send just one generic email or choose from dozens of templates, depending on the form used by the potential client or the information provided to the autoresponder by the potential client.

BING: A major search engine, like Google and Yahoo. It has many of the same features and has the next largest market share of any of the search engines after Google.

BLOG: Originally an abbreviation of the term "web log," it has now come to mean a type of website (or part of a website) that is frequently updated with new content and has many interactive options so that users can leave comments and otherwise participate. Many blogs are powered by software explicitly designed to make their frequent updating an easier and smoother process, like Wordpress or Typepad.

CALL TO ACTION: Content on a website or another method of communication which appeals to the reader to contact the business.

CRM: An acronym for "Customer Relationship Management." In the context of Internet marketing, it most often refers to the software put in place that manages clients and potential clients of the business, in other words, names, locations, likes, dislikes, needs, and other information that the business may find relevant.

DIRECTORY: In the sense of Internet marketing, a website or part of a website that lists businesses. Many of these, like Yelp, Merchant Circle, or CitySearch, also contain reviews of businesses which are often user-generated and submitted.

DUPLICATE CONTENT: Identical content that appears on multiple websites. Search engines have created ways of detecting this and often have algorithms that even detect if content has only been just slightly altered. Content that has just been altered slightly and is still virtually identical to the original content will be flagged as duplicate content by many search engines.

E-COMMERCE: The buying and selling of products and services over the Internet.

FACEBOOK: A social networking site that is currently the most popular in the world. It allows users to network with each other and socialize and share photos, thoughts and status updates as well as create "wall" posts with each other.

FACEBOOK PLACES: A specific segment of the social networking site Facebook. It allows users to see local spots around them as well as update their location in real time from mobile phones or other means, thus allowing other users to see where they are at any given time.

GEOLOCATION: In Internet marketing and SEO, a term used to describe location specific information, normally a city and state for most local businesses.

GOOGLE MAPS: A part of Google's website which primarily deals with maps and navigation. One of the features of Google Maps is the ability for local businesses to list themselves on it. The local search return feature was originally a part of this system before Google integrated it into the main search system after it proved to be so popular.

GOOGLE PLACES / GOOGLE + LOCAL: A part of Google's website which allows a business to have a specific page dedicated to them. It often hooks in with their location on Google Maps, and it features user-generated reviews of the business as well as links to other directories and review sites.

IP ADDRESS: A unique number that identifies a computer on a network. IP means Internet Protocol, the system for the transmission of data through “packets” of information.

KEYWORD: A term that a user searches with in a search engine to retrieve content that contains or is relevant to that term.

KEYWORD DENSITY: The use of a specific keyword present in any given piece of content. For example, given the keyword "racing" being used five times in a five hundred word blog post, the keyword density of "racing" would be 1%. Optimal keyword density is between 3 and 4% and should not exceed 4% or it can be flagged as spamming.

KEYWORD PHRASE / LONG TAIL KEYWORD PHRASE: A phrase comprised of multiple individual words, but treated like a single keyword for the purposes of a search, like "NASCAR car racing" or "racing opportunities in Texas."

KEYWORD RICH: Content that has many keywords and uses them often, with good keyword density.

KEYWORD TOOL: Tools created to help select optimal keywords for search engine marketing, like Google's Keyword Tool. They often contain information such as the amount of searches for a particular keyword or other metrics that help ascertain how popular or prevalent a given keyword or keyword phrase may be.

LINKEDIN: A social networking site that is geared towards businesses and professionals and enables them to link up and network more effectively.

LOCAL SEARCH RETURN: A feature within Google's search engine that returns location specific results for a user who types in keywords that relate to local businesses. For example, a local search return would appear for a user in Omaha, Nebraska, who typed in "check engine light" and show a map and the local businesses that are relevant to the search result in the ensuing search page.

NICHING: The practice of specializing a marketing strategy with a certain keyword or keyword phrase in order to rank in the highest spot in a local search return for that keyword or keyword phrase.

ROI: An acronym for "Return on Investment," which means the amount of profit or, in literal terms, the amount of money returned for the amount of money invested.

SEARCH ALGORITHM: A series of computer algorithms used by major search engines to index, search and rank websites on the Internet.

SEARCH ENGINE: A website or company, like Google, Bing, or Yahoo, which indexes other websites on the Internet and allows users to enter keywords in order to find relevant websites.

SEO: An acronym for "Search Engine Optimization." It refers to marketing that tries to increase exposure and gain clientele by using techniques and strategies to rank high on Internet search engines. It is often interchanged with SEM (Search Engine Marketing).

SOCIAL MEDIA: Sites whose primary purpose is to enable users to share content with each other and socialize on the Internet, sites like Facebook, Twitter, and LinkedIn.

SPAM: In Internet parlance, spam was originally used to refer to any unsolicited bulk messages sent over email. It is now also commonly used to refer to content on the Internet which is not useful, but is designed to make a page rank higher on search engines by tricking search engine algorithms into rating the content as higher quality than it actually is.

TWEET: An individual post on Twitter.

TWITTER: A social networking service that allows users to post 140 character tweets to their account with the ability for other users to follow them and respond to the tweets.

UNIQUE SELLING POSITION (USP): Unique Selling Position separates you from your competition in a specific market place. The term is often used to refer to any presentation that differentiates it from competitors.

URL: An acronym for "Uniform Resource Locator." It is the name that the user types into the browser bar in order to access a specific website, for example "www.google.com" or "www.bing.com."

BRING ME TO SPEAK AT YOUR NEXT EVENT

Want to bring the author to speak at your next event?

Bill Hawthorn's programs are designed to optimize the online marketing strategies of small businesses, especially local small businesses. His agency focuses on advanced SEO (Search Engine Optimization) and Local Searching as alternative means to traditional marketing.

His managing partners also conduct these educational sessions and altogether they have delivered over one thousand presentations around the USA and Canada.

They offer several different programs, including:

1) Websites, Google, and More: Getting Clients Online - the Ethics, Pitfalls and Techniques

2) Turning Clicks Into Clients: The Ultimate Presentation for Online Marketing

3) Social Media and Your Company: How to Leverage and Convert Clicks into New Clients with Facebook, Twitter, Linkedin and Google+

Inquire How You Can Book Us to Speak for FREE

Every year the publisher subsidizes Bill Hawthorn and his associates to speak to a limited number of groups and associations at no cost to them. To inquire about having us speak at your event for no additional charge contact us at: http://marketingsuccessfistappointment.com

BONUS

Discover Exactly How You Can Make a Few Slight Adjustments and Begin to Dominate Local Searches

It All Starts with Your 22 Point Review.

http://marketingsuccessfistappointment.com

If you want our valuable 22 Point Web Strategy Diagnosis, visit this link. There is no obligation on either your part or our part. This just begins a discussion about how we may be able to help you. This URL gives you a coupon that makes this $200 review free for you, since you are reading and implementing the things in this book.

Note, while it's free, we're busy, and availability may be limited, but it's a great opportunity to get your online presence reviewed by one of our experts.

While we know that some people take these experience-backed, high-quality web strategies and go and hire a cheap local marketing agency, we also know that the best customers -- those who understand the value of growing their business by maximizing their online marketing investment -- will ask us to just "do it for me."

We are always on the lookout for high quality clients to build a long-term relationship with. If that sounds like your business, then please feel free to write or call.

Phone: (203) 779-7400

Fax: (203) 774-1015

Web: http://marketingsuccessfistappointment.com

Or, text the keyword firstappointment, your name and your email to

58885

52001254R00066

Made in the USA
Charleston, SC
08 February 2016